A HISTORY

OF THE

COUNTY OF DU PAGE, ILLINOIS;

CONTAINING AN ACCOUNT OF

ITS EARLY SETTLEMENT AND PRESENT ADVANTAGES,

A SEPARATE

HISTORY OF THE SEVERAL TOWNS,

INCLUDING

NOTICES OF RELIGIOUS ORGANIZATIONS, EDUCATION, AGRICULTURE AND MANUFACTURES, WITH THE NAMES AND SOME ACCOUNT OF THE FIRST SETTLERS IN EACH TOWNSHIP,

AND MUCH

VALUABLE STATISTICAL INFORMATION.

By C. W. RICHMOND & H. F. VALLETTE.

CHICAGO:

:AM PRESSES OF SCRIPPS, BROSS & SPEARS, 45 CLARK STREET.

1857.

TO THE READER.

The authors propose to offer no apology for the appearance of this work. They are, however, conscious of many of its imperfections, to which it would be unwise in them to draw the attention of the public.

The original manuscript was prepared more than a year ago, and placed in the hands of a printer, whose establishment, with all his effects, including said manuscript, was carried down stream at the time of the high water last spring. To this circumstance may be attributed the delay in its publication, as well as some slight errors of omission and commission, which anybody is at liberty to find in the work. If the reader chances to discover anything of the kind, we here take the liberty to inform him beforehand, that "we knew it." And if anybody thinks he can write a better history of Du Page County, we can only say to him, in the

language of the good deacon who made an unsuccessful attempt to preach in the absence of the
regular pastor, " if you really think you can do it
better, why, try it, that's all."

We hereby tender our acknowledgments to the
following named persons, for much valuable in-
formation for the work: Capt. JOSEPH NAPER, Miss
NANCY HOBSON, JOHN WARNE, WILLARD SCOTT, R. N.
MURRAY, H. B. HILLS, H. D. FISHER, L. W. MILLS,
E. DUNCKLEE, Rev. Mr. WASHBURNE, E. R. LOOMIS,
Hon. WALTER BLANCHARD, JOHN GRANGER, MYRON
C. DUDLEY.

THE AUTHORS.

EARLY HISTORY OF THE COUNTY.

PIONEER REMINISCENCES.

THE present chapter is designed to embody the leading incidents connected with the early settlement of DU PAGE County, and embraces a period of nearly three years. It may be for the benefit of some to state, that this narrative does not disclose a succession of "disastrous chances," nor is it fraught with "moving accidents by flood and field," and he who peruses these pages, thinking to derive gratification from such sources, will undoubtedly be disappointed. The pioneers of our county are fast passing from us, and soon there will none remain to tell the story of their hardships.

That such facts and incidents, relating to their settlement here, as are considered worthy of record, may be preserved, is the object of this sketch; and if these convey no lessons of historic value, it is believed that they will not be devoid of interest to those familiar with the locality of the scenes described. The bulk of information herein detailed, has been gathered from authentic sources, from living witnesses; and if errors or omissions have occurred, the writer can only assert, in extenuation, the honesty of his intentions, and crave a liberal indulgence toward his deficiencies.

The first permanent settlement within the limits of Du Page, was made in the fall of 1830, and during the spring of the year following. Stephen J. Scott removed from Maryland to this State, with his family, in the year 1825, and "made a claim" near the present site of Gros Point. While on a hunting tour, in the month of August, 1830, in company with his son Willard, he discovered the Du Page river, near Plainfield. Impressed with the beauty and apparent fertility of the surrounding country, he resolved to explore the river, and ascended it as far as the confluence of its east and west branches, now called "The Forks." Here he became enamored of the gorgeous adornings with which the hand of nature had embellished the scene around him. In these he beheld infallible tokens of the "promised land," and it required but little time for him to ponder and determine the question of making that beautiful region his future home.

A comfortable log house was subsequently built upon the farm now owned by Mrs. Sheldon, and the family of Mr. Scott came on to possess the "new claim," in the fall of 1830. Other families soon settled in the vicinity. Although Mr. Scott is entitled to the distinction of having been the pioneer of the "settlement," which soon extended for several miles along the river into Will and Du Page, yet there are others who lay well established claims to the pioneership of this county. About the middle of March, 1831, Baley Hobson came and settled, with his family, near the present site of the family residence, being the first actual settler on the soil of Du Page County. The family of Mr. Paine located near Mr. Hobson, in April following. In July the family of Capt. Joseph Naper came from Ohio, accompanied by the family of his brother, John Naper. Capt. Naper had visited the county in February, 1831. He built a cabin near the site of his flouring mill, in which he lived until a more commodious dwelling could be provided for his family. He also built a trading house that season, and carried on quite an extensive trade with the settlers and Indians. The latter were quite numerous here at that time, but he always sustained the most friendly relations with them. The settlement received constant additions to its numbers, and at the end of spring, 1832, it contained one hundred and eighty souls. Among the families were those of H. T. Wilson, Lyman Butterfield, Ira Carpenter, John Murray, R. M. Sweet, Alanson Sweet, Harry Boardman, Israel Blodgett, Robert Strong, Pierce Hawley, Walter Stowel, C. Foster, J. Manning, and H. Babbitt.

The locality was then known as "Naper's Settlement." The winter of 1832 was one of unusual severity, which, together with a scarcity of provisions, rendered the prospects of the settlers rather gloomy. John Naper, John Murray, and R. M. Sweet were sent to the "Wabash" for provisions, from which place supplies were at length obtained, and the dreary season, "on his frozen wings," passed away without much suffering among the settlers. The new spring awoke and clothed the earth in all the beauty and freshness of a young creation, quickening into life countless germs, in bud, and flower, and tree; filling the air with the melody of motion, the murmur of released waters, and the song of birds, and spotting the verdure of the wide-spreading prairies with fire and gold in the tint of flowers. How true to the sentiment of all who witnessed the opening of that long looked for spring, must be the words of the poet:

" These are the gardens of the Desert — these
    The unshorn fields, boundless and beautiful,
    And fresh as the young earth ere man had sinned.
    The Prairies! I behold them for the first,
    And my heart swells, while the dilated sight
    Takes in the encircling vastness."

Never was a " good time come " hailed with more gladness than was the spring of 1832, by the infant colony. A prospect of reward for past hardships was before them. All was busy preparation for the approaching seed time. The labor of breaking and fencing went briskly forward, and in due time the new fledged grain came peering from the mellow ground. But long before the growing fields stood ready for the sickle of the glad harvester, the little band were obliged to relinquish their cherished anticipations, and flee from their new homes for the safety of their lives.

The news of the breaking out of the Black Hawk war caused great excitement in the settlement, and the alarm was heightened by the arrival of Shata, an express from the Pottawattomies, who were friendly to the whites, with the intelligence that a party of Sac Indians were committing depredations among the settlers on Fox river, some ten miles distant, and that the houses of

Cunningham and Hollenbeck had been burned to the ground, and their property entirely destroyed. Aware of their inability to carry on a successful warfare with the Indians, as the colony was in an almost defenseless state, and being liable to an attack from them at any moment, the settlers decided to send their families, with all possible haste, to Chicago, where old Fort Dearborn offered its protection to any fearing the incursions of the savages. The settlement was now the scene of universal disorder and alarm. Bustle and confusion were the order of the hour. Men were hurrying to and fro in eager pursuit of their wives and children, while weeping wives and crying children were hurrying with equal rapidity and greater anxiety in pursuit of their husbands and fathers. Order was at length, in some degree, restored, and while the women were engaged in packing such articles of clothing and provision as they would require for the journey, the men were actively fitting out teams to convey them away.

Early in the afternoon of the 18th of May, the train started for Chicago. But the family of Christopher Paine, who lived near the place of S. & D. Babbitt, consisting of his wife and six children, were, in the general confusion incident to their hasty departure, left behind. The family were sent in advance of the train, with directions to wait at a short distance from the settlement for its arrival. Concealing themselves in a thicket by the roadside, near the farm now owned by Capt. John Sargent, and not hearing the company as it passed, they were obliged to remain in their place of concealment during the night, which must have been

1*

one of fearful anxiety to the mother, as the imaginative dangers of her situation magnified, while watching over her houseless and defenseless children. They returned in safety to the settlement next morning, but much exhausted by fatigue and hunger.

The following incidents relating to the alarm and sudden flight of Mr. Hobson's family, have been kindly furnished by one of its members. Mr. Hobson, with Mr. Paine and son, had just seated themselves at their noonday meal, relating, in the meantime, the intelligence they had received while at work in the field; that a band of Indians were advancing, and were then only thirty miles distant, when they were suddenly interrupted by the appearance of Paine's eldest son, who rushed into the house, bareheaded and breathless, informing them that Specie and Ament had just arrived from the Au Sable grove, having run their horses down, and performed a part of the journey on foot, to bring the alarming intelligence that a body of Indians had that morning passed through Hollenbeck's grove, killing several settlers, and burning everything in their path. Upon this intelligence, immediate preparations for safety were considered expedient. Hobson and Paine arose from the table, leaving the dinner untasted. Mr. Paine, accompanied by his sons, started in great haste for their home, while Mr. Hobson prepared to ride up to the Naper settlement, to see what the inhabitants there had concluded to do, but his wife and children, clinging to him, begged him not to leave them; whereupon he saddled the horses, and after seeing the wife and children all mounted, except the eldest son, who was to accompany them on foot, they started together. They directed their course through the east end of the grove, and coming upon a rise of ground, beheld a man on horseback, about a mile distant. It immediately occurred to Mr. Hobson that this was an Indian spy, but it proved to be one of a small party of scouts, sent out from the settlement. He, however, directed his wife and children to hasten out of sight. They rode into the grove and dismounted. Mr. H. came up soon after, threw the saddles into a thicket, turned the horses into a neighboring field, and made all possible haste to secrete his family; directing them to use every precaution to evade pursuit, and not to tangle nor bruise the grass and weeds as they went along. Having done this, his attention was next directed to his dog, a faithful and valuable animal. "You have been," said he, "my companion and protector for years; you have never been unfaithful to a trust, nor given me cause to question your fidelity—always 'the first to welcome, foremost to defend.' But now you may betray us, and, saddening as the thought may be, I must be reconciled to the necessity of putting you to death." So, taking the unsuspecting victim, he went to a cabin near by, which had been but recently occupied by the family of Mr. Seth Wescott, his object being to procure an ax with which to do the deed at which his very soul shuddered. It was supposed that the family of Mr. Wescott had received the alarm, and fled. What then was his surprise to meet him at the threshold of his door, with gun in hand, just starting out on a hunting expedition. At Mr. Hobson's solicitation, the dog

was shot; but he died not, as many pass from life,
without a tear to consecrate the event, or a heart to
embalm the memory of the departed soul—his loss
was sincerely lamented. Mr. Wescott made immediate preparation to join the settlers, and Mr. Hobson,
fearing that the report of the gun might have alarmed
his family, hastened to meet them. Accompanied by
his wife he then returned to the house to make preparations, in case it should become necessary for them
to desert their home. The box had been removed
from the wagon, but with his wife's assistance he was
enabled to replace it, and, after completing their
arrangements, they again set forth, Mrs. Hobson with
some food to seek her children in the grove, while her
husband went to the settlement to see what preparations were being made there. On his arrival he found
that the families, with a part of the men, had gone to
Chicago. He informed those that remained of the
condition of his family, and of his anxiety that they
should set out that night, in hopes of overtaking the
advance party. Capt. Naper, Lieut. King, and Specie
volunteered to return with him to the place where he
had concealed his family. They were all mounted except King, who was on foot. Having found the family
in their hiding place, it was a matter that required
considerable mathematical skill to determine how they
were to be conveyed. It was at length decided that
the two eldest children should be placed on the horse
of Mr. Hobson; that Capt. Naper should take two
more on the horse with him; and that Mrs. Hobson,
assisted by King, should go on foot, carrying the
youngest child, then two years old. They pressed on

toward the north end of the grove, where Mr. Hobson had agreed to meet them with his team. Emerging from the grove they had yet half a mile to go, and Mrs. Hobson being fatigued by the journey, one of the children was taken from Capt. Naper's horse and placed on the horse with the two others, while Mrs. Hobson mounted behind Capt. Naper. They started again, one horse carrying Capt. Naper, with his huge Kentucky rifle, together with Mrs. Hobson, one child, and sundry and divers trappings. It is supposed that the gallant captain never presented a more formidable appearance than he did while riding along on that memorable occasion, with his burnished steel glistening in the moonbeams, although he has, since that day, been the hero of at least three decisive battles.

They arrived in safety at the place appointed to meet Mr. Hobson, who soon came up with his oxen and wagon, bringing with him such things from the house as he could hastily pick up in the dark. The announcement of "all aboard" soon followed. Mr. Hobson gave up his horse to Mr. King, who returned with Capt. Naper to the settlement, while the vehicle containing the family moved on its slow and weary way. The night was cold, and rendered still more uncomfortable by a heavy fall of rain; but wet and cold are of minor consideration, when compared with the horrors of an excited imagination, which transforms every tree and shrub into a merciless Indian foe, with tomahawk and scalping knife in hand, ready to commit their deeds of cruelty and slaughter. Passing a night of the most intense fear and anxiety, they arrived at Brush Hill at sunrise. Crossing the

O'Plain, they found a habitation, the only one on the
whole route. They journeyed on, and soon reached
the "Big Prairie," the distance across which is about
ten miles. Crossing this prairie was the most tedious
part of the way. The wheels, during a greater part
of the distance, were half imbedded in the marshy
soil, rendering it almost impossible for the team to
move on, even with an empty wagon. The children
became sickened from exposure and thirst. Being
unprovided with a drinking vessel, Mrs. Hobson frequently took the shoe from her foot and dipped the
muddy water from the pools by the roadside, which
they drank with much apparent satisfaction. They
plodded on at a slow pace, and reached their destination at a little before sunset, much exhausted by
hunger and fatigue, neither Mr. nor Mrs. Hobson
having tasted food for more than thirty-six hours.
They were safely quartered in Fort Dearborn, and
here we leave them, and return to the settlement.

Some fifteen or twenty men remained behind, when
the settlement was abandoned by the families, in order
to protect, if possible, their dwellings and other property, from the depredations of the Indians, should they
come to destroy them. They quartered themselves in
the log house of Capt. Naper, and kept vigilant guard
during the night. On the following morning the settlement was visited by Lawton, an Indian trader, living on the O'Plain, in company with three Indians
and a half-breed, named Burrasaw. They brought no
news, but came to gather further particulars in relation to the threatened invasion of the Sacs. As the
settlers had heard nothing of their movements since

the departure of Shata's express, it was resolved that a party, joined by Lawton and the three Indians, should go to the camp of the Pottawattomies, near the Big Woods, some ten miles distant, for information. Two men, named Brown and Murphy, had been placed on patrol that morning, and were out on the prairie, a little west of the settlement. The party setting out for the Big Woods determined to test their courage, and for that purpose, sent the three Indians in advance of the main party. As soon as the Indians came in sight of the patrol, they gave a most terrific war whoop, and darted on after them with the fleetness of so many arrows. The patrol, seized with sudden consternation, sprang to their horses and fled in the wildest dismay—first toward the north, but being intercepted by some of the company, whom they took to be savages, they wheeled and took an opposite direction. In this course they were again intercepted by the three Indians. Concluding they must be surrounded, they came to a halt, laid down their arms, and were about to sue for mercy, when they chanced to discover in the features of their vengeful pursuers a striking likeness to those they had left at the settlement. The fact soon dawned upon them that they had been successfully hoaxed, and their duties "on guard" terminated with that adventure.

The company advanced toward the Big Woods. As they drew near the timber, an Indian was observed mounted on a horse, who, on seeing them, turned and fled. The three Indians made instant pursuit; overtaking him before he had gone far, they made themselves known as friends, and detained him

until the company came up. Lawton understood the
dialects of several Indian tribes, and in a conversation
with him ascertained that he belonged to the Pottawattomies, who were encamped only three miles
distant. The Indian said the whole of his tribe were
drunk, and it would be dangerous for the company
to visit them. However, after brief consultation, they
decided to proceed to the encampment, and the
captured Indian led the way. Although the appearance of the company in the camp, caused some little
excitement among that portion of the tribe who were
sufficiently sober to entertain an emotion of any kind,
yet they were received with no apparent indications
of hostility. On examination, the testimony of the
Indian was fully substantiated. Indians were found
in a state of beastly intoxication in every part of the
camp; while others were enjoying the pastime in the
most picturesque, amusing and fantastic series of per-
formances that can be imagined. Dancing, singing,
whooping and screeching, delightfully mingled, formed the grand offering which there went up at the
shrine of bad whisky and worse tobacco. One
fellow, who seemed to be of a decidedly pugnacious
turn, was lying on the ground, face downwards, with
his hands secured behind him, Samson like, with
green withes. Frantic with rage, he seemed to utter
the most vehement and fearful denunciations against
all who came near him. Upon inquiry, it was ascertained that the fellow had violated an important law
in their code respecting these orgies, which law for-
bids " a brother knocking a brother down," and he
was suffering the penalty affixed.

The company were summoned into the presence of the chiefs, who gave them a friendly and courteous reception. A council was called, and Lawton and Burrasaw were admitted to the ring. The consultation lasted for two or three hours, and the "outsiders" were becoming rather impatient. An old Indian woman, known to Capt. Naper, while passing near him, uttered in his ear the word " Puc-a-che," which, being both literally and liberally interpreted, signifies " Be off." And the Captain began to think it time to heed the advice.

Inquiry was made in relation to the deliberations of the council, and Lawton responded, that " there were three hundred Sac Indians in the Black Berry timber, some four miles distant; and," said he, "you will see them if you wait here an hour. These Indians will not fight them, but will 'stop them by talk,' if they can, from burning your settlement." The Captain signified no inclination to hold an interview with three hundred Sac Indians, but suggested the propriety of retreating to the settlement as soon as possible, and sending the most valuable property there to Chicago. This plan received the acquiescence of all the company, and after making arrangements with Lawton to send an express to notify them of any immediate danger from the Sacs, the settlers returned. The packing of their goods was immediately commenced. All the articles which were inconvenient to convey, were lowered into a well partly dug, and all was soon ready for loading the wagons. The horses had been harnessed, and were then feeding at a stable some ten or fifteen rods from the house.

Capt. Naper was in the house tying the corners of a quilt, which contained the remnant of clothing left behind by his family, when a man rushed wildly into the room, shouting at the top of his voice, "the Indians are upon us!" The whole company took instant alarm, and with the exception of Captain and John Naper, beat a precipitate retreat to a thicket of hazel bushes, which, in those days, flourished in prolific exuberance on the soil now known as Jefferson avenue. The two Napers were somewhat unlike the redoutable Mr. Sparrowgrass, who was prone to pull trigger and make inquiries afterward. They decided that *inquiry* should take the precedence, and if it came to that, why, they could *run some*.

As the horses were near, they removed the harness and put on the saddles, that they might be in readiness in case of emergency. They had scarcely accomplished this, when Alanson Sweet came galloping up on his fierce charger, exhorting them to instant flight, if they valued their lives. "There are at least five hundred Indians upon us," said he, "and they are not more than fifteen rods off." Alanson rode away, but the Napers resolved to investigate. They walked in the direction from which Sweet said the Indians were approaching, and soon came upon a rise of ground which had concealed the Indians from view, when lo! the dusky visage of their friend Lawton appeared before them. He was at the head of about fifty brawny Pottawattomies, and had come to warn the settlers of immediate danger. Messengers were sent out to gather in the fugitives, that all might listen to Lawton's story. He said that at least sixteen of the Sacs, and how many

more he did not know, had crossed Fox river; that
the Pottawattomies could not stop them. They were
determined to attack the settlements, and their "talk"
could not prevent them. The settlers, upon this, abandoned all idea of saving their property, but determined
to make every effort to save the wife and children of
Paine, who were still in the settlement. The horses
were attached to a light covered wagon, in which the
family was placed, and the whole company set out that
night for Chicago. John Naper insisted upon going
on foot, and divested himself of everything in the
shape of attire, except his shirt and pantaloons. He
was earnestly entreated to ride, but upon his assuring
the party that "he could outrun any Sac Indian in
the nation," further importunity was deemed useless.
They reached the O'Plain, and encamped for the night
without taking their horses from the wagon, that they
might be ready to move on at a moment's warning.
They had hastened on, through fear of being cut off
on the northern trail, by the Indians, and being much
worn with fatigue, all hands slept pretty soundly till
next morning. The journey was then resumed, and
the party arrived at Chicago before noon, on the 20th
day of May. A company of twenty-five men was
raised during the day, to return to the settlement. It
consisted chiefly of settlers, accompanied by Captain
Brown and Colonel Hamilton. They started on Saturday, May 21st, and passed the night at Lawton's.
Next day they went on to the settlement, where they
found everything undisturbed. Leaving the settlement under the guardianship of several friendly
Indians, the company proceeded to Plainfield, where

they found the settlers safely quartered in a fort, which they had just completed. They then started for Holderman's grove, to ascertain the condition of the settlers there. Meeting Cunningham and Hollenbeck on the way, they were informed that it would be of no use to go further, as their property had been destroyed. Notwithstanding, they proceeded to Holderman's grove. From this place they sent an express to Ottawa, to notify the settlers of the safety of their property, and also sent a messenger to Chicago, to apprise their friends of their own safety. The party remained at Holderman's house during the night. Early next morning the express returned from Ottawa, bringing the intelligence of the massacre at Indian creek. The party immediately went to Ottawa, and thence proceeded to the scene of the bloody tragedy. What they there witnessed was too appalling to be described. Not less than fifteen bodies, of men, women, and children, were lying there, cut and mangled in the most shocking manner. It was ascertained that they were of the families of Messrs. Hall, Davis and Pettigrew, and that two daughters of the Hall family, Silvia and Rachel, the one about seventeen and the other about fifteen years old, were carried off as prisoners. The party of Indians immediately retreated into the Winnebago country, up Rock river, carrying the scalps of the slain and their prisoners with them. "Indian wars are the wars of a past age. They have always been characterized by the same ferocity and cruelty. To describe this massacre is only to repeat what has been written a hundred times; but a brief account of it may not be deemed inappropriate in this place. The Indians were about seventy in number. They approached the house in which the three families were assembled in the day time. They entered it suddenly, with but little notice. Some of the inmates were immediately shot down with rifles, others were pierced through with spears or despatched with the tomahawk. The Indians afterward related, with an infernal glee, how the women had squeaked like geese when they were run through the body with spears, or felt the sharp tomahawk entering their heads. All the victims were carefully scalped, their bodies shockingly mutilated; the little children were chopped to pieces with axes, and the bodies of the women were suspended by the feet from the walls of the houses. The young women prisoners were hurried, by forced marches, beyond the reach of pursuit. After a long and fatiguing journey with their Indian conductors, through a wilderness country, with but little to eat, and being subject to a variety of fortune, they were at last purchased by the chiefs of the Winnebagoes, employed by Mr. Gratiot for the purpose, with two thousand dollars, in horses, wampum, and trinkets, and were returned in safety to their friends."

The company assisted in burying the dead, and returned with sad hearts to Ottawa. There they found Col. Stillman's command, consisting of about two hundred men, under Col. Johnson. The settlers, or Capt. Brown's company, as it was called, encamped on the north side of the river, near where the city of Ottawa now stands. Capt. Brown's company being so small, he requested Col. Johnson to send an escort with his party to Chicago, as it was expected that they would be at-

tacked by Indians on their return. Col. Johnson refused
to send men for that purpose, but paraded his company
and called for volunteers. Maj. Bailey and twelve
privates volunteered to go. But the company being
still very small, Col. Johnson agreed to send a detach-
ment up the river and meet Maj. Brown's company
at Green's mill. Upon this assurance, the settlers left
Ottawa and followed the river up as far as Green's,
but no tidings came to them of Col. Johnson's detach-
ment. Returning to Holderman's grove, they found
everything laid waste. The settlement there was a
scene of complete devastation and ruin. They proceeded to Plainfield, and found the garrison in a state
of great alarm, occasioned by the news of the massacre at Indian creek. The women, who appeared
the more courageous, provided the company with a
good supper, and they remained there until next day.
In the morning the settlement was abandoned, and all
started for Chicago, except a preacher by the name of
Paine. He refused to accompany them, as he had,
from some cause, conceived the notion that the settlers
at Chicago had all been murdered. He started in the
direction of Holderman's grove, but was found murdered some days afterward, with one scalp torn from
his head and another from his face. Paine was wont
to wear a very heavy beard, which accounts for the
scalp being taken from his face. There is a tradition
of this brutal affair, which informs us that the Indians
cut off Paine's head and carried it with them, supposing, from the appearance given to the face by its long
beard, that they had killed one of the gods of the
whites.

The settlers all reached Chicago the same day on which they left Plainfield.

The Scott families, which should have been noticed in another place, did not abandon their claims at the Forks, until some time after the inhabitants fled from the settlement. A son of Robinson, an Indian chief of the Pottawattomie tribe, was living with them, and they knew that, in case of actual danger from the Sacs, the boy would be taken away. When he was removed, they concluded there would be no safety in remaining longer, and thereupon followed in the trail of their affrighted neighbors, to Fort Dearborn.

Not long after, a scouting party of twenty-five horsemen started for the settlement; their object being to ascertain whether any of the enemy had been there, and to look after the property of the settlers. This expedition was placed under the command of Col. B. Beaubien. They left Chicago in the morning, and at noon reached the O'Plain river, where they found Robert Kinzie, with fifty Indians under his command.

An arrangement was made, by which it was agreed that the Indians, under Captain Kinzie, should proceed by the direct trail to the settlement, and the mounted company should proceed to the same place by way of Capt. Boardman's, to look after the property there.

It was expected that the latter party would arrive at the settlement some time before the former. Beaubien's company urged their horses on as fast as possible, and in a few hours arrived at Ellsworth's grove. The skirt of timber, which then extended over nearly the whole area of the present village of Naperville, concealed the settlement from their view, but to their surprise, and we might add, to the dismay of some, smoke was seen rising from the place where Naper's house was situated. A halt was called, and by some of the company, most willingly obeyed. A hasty consultation followed, and John Naper, who was ever ready to "don armor and break a lance" in the cause of his friends, volunteered to ride around the point of timber, and ascertain whether the settlement was in the possession of friend or foe. In case he should meet with friends, he was to discharge his rifle, to notify his waiting and anxious comrades of that fact. But if foes were encountered, he was to return immediately to the company. His progress was watched with no small degree of interest, until he passed behind the point of timber, out of sight. Soon the reports of *two* guns were heard, and Naper did not make his appearance. In all probability he was shot, and the alarm among the company increased. There was no means of telling how numerous the enemy might be, nor how soon the sharp report of the rifle might be their own death-knell.

Two of the company, one of whom was mounted on a pack mule, and the other on a diminutive pack pony, belonging to the American Fur Company, manifested considerable uneasiness, as they had found by actual experience that neither of their animals was very remarkable for speed, and knew that in case of flight they must inevitably fall in the rear, and become an easy prey to their pursuers. They considered discretion as the better part of valor, and "self-preserva-

tion the first law of nature,'" and, suiting their action
to the consideration, hobbled off toward the East
Branch timber. They had not gone far when they
were discovered by Col. Beaubien, who rode on after
them, loudly vociferating, "Halt! halt!" They did
not heed the command, but concentrated all their
efforts to get out of his way. Beaubien put spurs to
his horse and soon ran them down. Coming up to
them he drew a pistol, and, presenting it, uttered the
effective condition and conclusion, "You run? By
gar! you run, me shoot you!" The argument was
irresistable, and the fugitives were captured and
brought back. R. N. Murray, who was with the
company, being well mounted, started to go and ascertain what had become of Naper; but he had gone only
a short distance when John made his appearance and
gave the signal that friends were in the camp; which
signal was greeted with a shout as joyous as any that
ever broke the silence of that grove. On entering the
settlement it was ascertained that the Indians under
Capt. Kinzie had accomplished the journey before
them, and had fired the two guns as a salute to the
gallant Naper, as he rode fearlessly into the camp.
The company had been out all day, and were very
hungry, but nothing could be found at the settlement in the way of provisions. Among the cattle
feeding on the prairie was a fine, fat steer, belonging
to R. M. Sweet, and it was decided that it should be
slaughtered for their evening's repast. The cattle
were all very wild, and ran off in fright whenever
they were approached, so that the only method of
securing the young steer was by shooting it. The

2

Indians being anxious to undertake this part of the project, about fifty of them were provided with rifles, and they sallied forth toward the place where the herd was feeding, capering and cutting all kinds of antics as they went along. As they approached the herd their victim was singled out, and two or three shots were fired without taking effect. The affrighted animal ran bellowing over the field, closely pressed by his assailants, who kept up a continual fire upon him, until the whole round had been discharged.

Of the fifty shots directed toward the animal, none proved mortal. A rifle ball, however, more fatally lodged, sent a tremor through his frame, and caused him to slacken his pace. The chase continued for some time, when the animal, in attempting to cross a slough, became mired and was easily taken. "War seemed a civil game," compared to the uproar that followed the fall of this hero. And as they bore him upon their shoulders triumphantly into the camp, one would have supposed, from the infernal yelling and screeching of those Indians, which

> "Embowel'd with outrageous noise the air,"

that Milton's deep-throated engines were again let loose with a certainty. They all shared the triumph, and each celebrated the capture of the steer as his own special achievement. Nothing could exceed the vainglorious vaporing of these rude sons of the forest, as they strutted about and exulted in the heroism of the adventure. The animal was properly dressed, and portions of the meat were prepared for supper, of which all partook with a good degree of relish.

After supper the log store was broken open and found to contain, among other things, a good supply of the two staple articles of pioneer merchandise, viz.: rum and tobacco. These were dealt out profusely to the Indians as a reward for their *valorous* conduct in the evening chase. The company remained at the settlement during the night. In the evening, to vary the monotony a little, they prevailed upon the Indians to get up a war dance. This performance, when dramatically considered, is strictly tragic, but it must be admitted that the "bill" for that evening had a fair sprinkling of the comic. Scalping scenes and tomahawk scenes were presented in the most approved Indian fashion, to the infinite amusement of a small but "highly respectable audience." At a late hour the whole company *retired*, each individual selecting his "site" without respect to the complexion of his neighbor.

In the morning the company under Beaubien arose with an impatient desire to meet the enemy. They had slept off the fatigue of the previous day, and their desire for conflict returned with redoubled force with the restoration of their bodily energies. They resolved upon committing havoc among the Sacs, and fearing that they might, in some unguarded moment, slay some of their friends, the Pottawattomies, by mistake, they went again to the old log store and procured a piece of cotton sheeting, which they tore into small strips and tied around the head and waist of each friendly Indian. Thus decorated, they left the party of Capt. Kinzie, and started for the Big Woods. The prairies were scoured, but not an Indian, nor trace of an Indian, was to be found.

The company returned to the settlement sadly
dejected at the ill success of their Quixotic adventure, and started for Chicago on the following morning. Nothing transpired on the way worthy of notice,
except that the company rode as far as Brush Hill
constantly expecting to suffer the inconvenience of
being shot, through the carelessness of one of its
members, a young man then fresh from New York
City, but now an individual of some distinction in
Chicago City. He accidentally discharged his piece
three times before reaching Brush Hill. The guns
were strapped to the saddles in a horizontal position,
and the chances were that the young man's random
shots would take effect, if he was allowed the range
of the whole company much longer. Arriving at
Brush Hill and attempting to dismount, bang! went
his gun again. This aroused the ire of Col. Beaubien.
He could endure it no longer, and commanded the
youth to surrender up his arms. This the young man
stoutly refused to do, whereupon Col. Beaubien made
a violent descent upon him, threw him down, and
after a short struggle succeeded in wresting the gun
from his grasp, after which there was no more "firing
on parade" that day.

A short time after, Capt. Naper, Capt. H. Boardman,
and some ten or twelve others, went out from Chicago
to the settlement to examine the crops. Nothing had
been disturbed, and the crops were found in good
condition. From the settlement they went to Ottawa,
to obtain from Gen. Atkinson, who was stationed there
with about fifty men, assistance to build a fort at the
Naper settlement. Gen. Atkinson dispatched the
company under Capt. Paine at Joliet, to aid them in

the enterprise. They proceeded to the Naper settlement and erected a fort near the house of Lewis Ellsworth, and in honor of the captain of the company dispatched to aid them, called it Fort Paine. The fort was built of pickets, with two block houses, and so constructed that it could be defended from an attack on either side. An incident occurred just before the completion of this fort, which threw a gloom over the minds of the settlers, and excited fears which had been entirely allayed by the prospect of a speedy protection. Two men, named Brown and Buckley, were sent to Sweet's grove to procure a load of shingles. They had gone as far -as the grove, north of the Beaubien place, when Buckley got out of the wagon to open a passage in the fence. Brown drove through into the field, and the team continued to move on, while Buckley walked leisurely along behind. Suddenly the sharp report of a rifle was heard from an adjoining thicket, and Buckley saw his comrade fall dead from the wagon. Terrified and bewildered he fled toward the settlement. He reached the fort with scarcely strength to communicate the melancholy tidings to his sorrowing companions. About twenty men left the fort and proceeded to the scene of the disaster. The horses had been stripped of their harness and taken away, and the body of Brown was found near the wagon, pierced with three balls. It was brought to the fort and buried. The trail of the Indians was followed, but they had fled beyond the reach of pursuit.

As much alarm now prevailed throughout the company, it was decided that Capt. Naper and

Alanson Sweet, should start that night for Chicago
to procure more men. They started on horseback,
but Sweet's horse giving out, he was obliged to
journey on foot. An incident occurred during this
trip, which strikingly exhibits the force of a capri-
cious imagination, and the liability to deception when
that faculty is unduly excited. They were approaching Flag creek, when Sweet affirmed that he saw two
Indians, one on foot and the other on horseback, and
proposed to let Capt. Naper go on with his horse
while he concealed himself in the grass. The Captain's attention was directed to the objects, and they
bore the same appearance to him. He requested
Sweet to mount behind him, that they might both
move toward them. He did so, and they rode on.
As they passed along, the path deviated to the right,
and the objects began to separate. This confirmed
them in their impression, and Sweet declared that
they were Indians, for he could see them move.
After going several rods they turned and rode back
the same path, and then the objects began to approach
each other, and when they had arrived at the place
where Sweet mounted, the *Indians* had resumed
their first position. This little experiment convinced
them of their delusion, and they rode bravely on.
The objects were found to be two trees of different
heights, a mile distant, and half a mile apart. They
reached Chicago early next morning, and asked assistance from Gen. Williams, who was there with three
hundred troops from Michigan, but he refused to furnish it, as he did not deem it safe to send men into
the country at that time. At length Maj. Wilson

informed Capt. Naper, that if Gen. Williams would consent, he would take some of his men and return with him to the settlement. Whereupon, a council of officers was held, but it was deemed unsafe for any to go, even as volunteers. Capt. Naper then left Chicago and returned much disheartened to the settlement.

There being no better alternative, the settlers resolved to remain where they were, and acting wisely upon this resolution, placed themselves in the best possible position for defense. Scouting parties were frequently sent out to range the surrounding country, but no skirmishes were had with the Indians. The nearest approach to an encounter with the enemy took place on the Fourth of July. Fired with the patriotic spirit which animated the sires of Seventy-Six, a small party shouldered their muskets, and set forth to scour the surrounding country in pursuit of adventure. After a fatiguing day's march the party arrived at the Au Sable grove, without having an opportunity for the slightest display of their pent-up valor. Here they encamped for the night. After supper they drew around the camp fire, and John Naper became the oracle of the evening. His anecdotes and tales of adventurous deeds and noble daring, kept the whole party wide awake and in good cheer far into the night, when the "meeting" broke up, and deep sleep soon assumed the sovereignty of the camp. In the morning breakfast was prepared, and after enjoying the repast preparations were being made to depart. Willard Scott, who from early associations had become skilled in backwoods craft,

and regarded every track with the knowing eye of an
Indian, was a member of the company. As they
were about to leave the place, he discovered what
appeared to him to be a fresh Indian trail, and upon
further examination decided, that two Indians accompanied by a boy had recently passed near the encampment. This intelligence aroused the depressed spirits
of the whole party, and all were eager for pursuit.
The trail was followed with some difficulty to the
river bank, opposite the village encampment of the
Pottawattomies. Here from certain indications on
the stones and sand, Mr. Scott knew the Indians had
crossed the stream. A council of war was now held,
and the plan adopted of crossing and riding rapidly
up the opposite bank, and if the Indians were then in
view they could be easily surprised and taken. The
word for starting was given, and a general stampede
ensued. John Naper was the first to reach the
opposite bank and announce that the Indians were in
sight. They were standing upon the roof of a
wigwam, evidently watching for the direction of their
pursuers. As soon as John made his appearance they
leaped quickly to the ground, made off toward the
river and were soon out of sight. The party hastened
to the spot and followed their trail to the river. They
had evidently crossed to the opposite bank, and the
party recrossed in pursuit, but no further trace of
their progress could be found. After making diligent
search, and having abandoned all hope of again finding the trail, the company sat down and partook of
some refreshments from their knapsacks, and soon
after made their way back to the settlement, some-

what chagrined at being compelled to surrender to the artifice of their wily fugitives. The Indians eluded them by crossing to a small island in the stream, upon which was a cluster of trees. Having climbed one of the tallest trees and concealed themselves among its branches, they sat and viewed the maneuvers of their vanquished pursuers with the greatest glee. They afterward related the whole affair to Robinson, a chief of the Pottawattomies, and arrogated to themselves a vast amount of credit for having so successfully eluded the sharp eye of "White Eagle," an appellation which they applied to Mr. Scott. This title originated from the following circumstance: Mr. David McKee, an acquaintance of Mr. Scott, had, in his deal with the Indians, received a buck-skin coat from one of them as a pledge for certain goods sold to him. A time at which the coat was to be redeemed was fixed by the parties, but when it arrived the Indian did not make his appearance, and the coat therefore became the property of Mr. McKee. It was subsequently sold to Mr. Scott.

Several months after, Mr. McKee, having occassion to visit an Indian settlement near Racine, for the purpose of trading with them, Mr. Scott accompanied him. Among the Indians in the settlement, they found the one from whom McKee had received the coat. Seeing the article in Mr. Scott's possession, he instantly demanded that it should be given up. He was told that he could have it by paying the sum for which it was left in pledge, but this he refused to do, at the same time persisting in his demand for an unconditional surrender of the garment. Upon re-

2*

ceiving a peremptory refusal, he threatened to take it by force. This considerably aroused the ire of Mr. Scott, and he told him, that if he wanted the coat, he might try the expediency of taking it from him. Upon this, the Indian left them, threatening him with great vengeance, and promising to return immediately with a sufficient force to take the coat from his back.

He soon returned, accompanied by some fifty or sixty of his companions, all fully armed, and painted in the most barbarous manner. Their appearance was enough to terrify any one who was unaccustomed to the stratagems to which Indians resort to carry their ends. As they approached, Scott and McKee gathered up their arms, and stood in a defensive attitude, confronting the whole party. The Indian who claimed the coat advanced and demanded it, threatening their destruction if again refused. Mr. Scott boldly informed him that the coat was on his back, and if he wanted it he must take it off. In the mean time, a young Indian chief, who was acquainted with the circumstances of the case, came and took a position with them, saying that he would stand by them in any emergency. The Indians then set up a most unearthly howling, and continued for some time to dance around them, flourishing their tomahawks, and trying to intimidate them with the most awful threats and frightful grimaces. At last, finding their efforts to obtain the coat unavailing, they withdrew, leaving Scott and McKee in full possession of the field. From that day afterward they always addressed Mr. Scott as "White Eagle," a title which belonged to none but the bravest. Although the stand taken by the young Indian chief in their favor may have saved them their lives, yet it is not supposed that the Iudians designed to do anything more than to frighten them into a surrender of the coat.

Mr. Scott, from a long intercourse with them, had become pretty well inured to their trickery, and was not easily deceived by appearances. He had lived among them and hunted with them, until he came to look upon many of their "signs and tokens" with considerable credulity. Among other practices, common among these Indians, was that of leaving pipes filled with tobacco in certain places on their hunting grounds, whenever they had bad luck, that the Great Spirit might come and smoke, by which they supposed his favor was secured, and that they would consequently have more favorable fortune. This device was employed by Mr. Scott, on *one* occasion, with marked success. A company started from the settlement for an afternoon's foray in the East Branch timber. It was a luckless expedition, and night came on, finding them entirely destitute of game. Between sundown and dark the hunters assembled to set out together for the settlement. Mr. Scott now produced his pipe, filled it with tobacco, applied a match to it, and placed it very mysteriously in the crotch of a tree. The party started, Mr. Scott riding some distance in the rear of the main body. He had not gone far when a beautiful, fat deer sprang from a thicket and crossed the path just before him. He leveled his rifle, and sent a ball whizzing through its heart. Before his gun was fairly loaded, another appeared, which met the same fate. The report of his rifle brought back the main party, who, upon witnessing the feat he had performed, were no

longer inclined to ridicule the idea of feeding the
"Great Spirit" with tobacco.

About this time Messrs. Hobson, Goodwin, Boardman, and Strong, were returning from Chicago with
two ox teams. Hobson and Goodwin were riding in
one wagon, and Boardman and Strong in the other.
It was a warm summer's day, and Strong laid down in
the wagon and fell asleep. Discovering that his companion was taking a nap, and ever on the *qui vive* for
a little fun, Boardman called to Hobson to come and
fire his gun near Strong's head, and see what the effect
would be. Hobson brought his gun and discharged it
as directed, when Strong, suddenly awakened by the
report, and supposing himself beset with Indians, made
a desperate attempt to go down through the bottom
boards of the wagon box. The joke was now on
Strong, and after the "laugh" had subsided, they
drove on. By and by Strong concluded to try Hobson's courage. A plan was secretly devised between
him and Goodwin, by which Strong was to secrete
himself in a thicket some distance ahead, and when
Hobson came along, get up some demonstrations that
would lead him to think that there were Indians there.
As Hobson's team approached the place, the war whoop
was sounded, and one or two shots fired. Goodwin
manifested extreme terror, and seizing both guns, ran
off, leaving Mr. Hobson alone, with nothing to defend
himself but an ox whip. But he was not to be intimi-
dated, and, without altering his course, rode past the
thicket, standing erect in his wagon, with a fixed and
searching look upon the place from which the "mani-
festations" proceeded.

Strong abandoned the idea of attempting again to frighten Hobson, and Goodwin was coolly informed, that if he ever meddled with Hobson's rifle again, he would stand the chance of getting his own brains blowed out.

Of the condition of the families at Fort Dearborn nothing has yet been said. We have been informed by some who went there, that it seemed as though they were to be shut up to starve, if not to be slaughtered by the Indians, having, in their hasty flight, taken but a scant supply of provisions, and there being little or nothing to be had in Chicago. For a time the garrison was supplied with beef by Claybourne, who was employed to butcher for the Pottawattomies by government, but the meat was so poor that necessity alone could have compelled them to use it. Among the families in the fort was that of a Mr. Harris, who lived at Hollenbeck's grove. At the time of the alarm, the father of Mrs. Harris, a very aged man, was too feeble to make his escape unassisted. He begged them to leave him and make *their* escape, if possible, saying that if the Indians killed him, they would only rob him of a few years. He was left alone, and four days elapsed before they were enabled to return, prepared to remove him. The Indians had visited the house in the mean time, but did not attempt to molest him, nor anything about the premises. When the regular troops came on from Michigan, the settlers were ordered to quit the fort, and every hovel that would afford a shelter was immediately crowded with occupants. At this time there were several women and children in the fort whose husbands and fathers were at the Naper settlement, building the fort there. These would have been turned out of doors, had it not been for the entreaty and expostulation of the volunteer company. By an exceedingly *liberal* provision, Mrs. Hawley and six children, Mrs. Blodgett and four children, and Mrs. Hobson and five children, were allowed to occupy an upper room in the establishment, about ten feet square. Any one can calculate the space occupied by each for a bed. Here they remained for ten days, before they could make their situation known to their husbands. The Indians did not appear near the fort at any time during their stay, although the garrison was one day thrown into great excitement by a false alarm. This afforded an opportunity to test the courage of the inmates, who, with one exception, proved undaunted. It is said that a gentleman who made bravery his boast, was missing for six or eight hours after the alarm, when he was found snugly ensconced under a feather-bed, but in a state of great trepidation.

In July the command of Gen. Scott passed on to Dixon, and the main army soon followed. With the government troops between them and their foe, the settlers had no further cause to fear. The families were brought back from Fort Dearborn, and placed in and near the fort—those of Mr. Scott, Capt. Boardman, Mr. Hobson, and John Naper, occupying a log house near by. Here they remained without molestation until after the battle of Bad Axe, which put an end to the Black Hawk war. This took place in September. All apprehension of danger was now at an end. The settlers resumed their claims, and, in uninterrupted peace and prosperity, many of them have lived to enjoy the abundant fruits of their valiant pioneership.

OLD "CLAIM FEUDS," ETC.

AFTER the close of the Black Hawk war, the tide of immigration again turned to Illinois, and this county received its proportion of new settlers.

The first settlers selected, of course, the best loca- tions, which were adjacent to the timber. The upland, or dry prairie, was usually selected in preference to the low and wet, and especially preferred wherever good facilities for obtaining water were offered.

The houses of the first settlers were usually built near the timber. Scarcely any were to be found upon the prairie prior to 1837. All the timber land was "claimed" before 1835, but some of the prairie land in our county, which, at that day, was considered almost worthless, on account of its being inconvenient to tim- ber, was never claimed by the squatters. Many diffi- culties arose among the settlers in relation to the boundaries and priority of the claims of parties.

Troubles of this kind are incident to the early set- tlement of any country, where the settlement precedes the survey of the land by government. The difficulties here, as elsewhere, created bitter feelings of animosity between neighbors, and, in too many instances, these feelings have not been allayed even to the present day; and we often hear disparaging remarks made by one respecting another, which, when traced to their origin, are found to emanate from the old "claim feuds." Nor were these quarrels confined to words alone. Many bloody combats occurred between belligerent parties; the one being usually the first claimant, the other, one who had "jumped the claim." Although blood was freely spilled during these contests, yet, with the exception of but one instance, which will be referred to hereafter, no lives were sacrificed. Sometimes the party in the wrong was driven from the field by the rightful claimant, assisted by his neighbors; for in those days the laws of Judge Lynch were often executed in a summary manner. An understanding, or implied agreement, existed among the settlers, that those who obtained portions of the claims of others by preëmption, or by purchase at the land sale, should deed to such claimant the part belonging to him. This was called an agreement to "deed and redeed." Most of the land was claimed by those who intended to purchase it, and make a permanent home for themselves and their families. Some of it, however, was claimed by what were then called "land sharks." This class of men merely claimed the land for the purpose of selling it to subsequent settlers, and were not usually protected in their claims by those who were always ready to assist a *bona fide* settler. The claims often sold for prices which would, even now, be considered exorbitant for the land. A few of the land sharks made money by their swindling operations, but most of them can boast of but little wealth at the present time, as they were of that class who spend their money as readily as they obtain it, and engage in speculations more wild and more dishonorable than stealing land, even, from actual settlers.

A company was formed somewhere in this county, between 1832 and 1835, which was called—for what reason we know not—"The Land Pirate Company." This company made, or caused to be made, a claim in the Big Woods, embracing three or four sections of the best timbered land. Their claim was inclosed with a rail fence, some two or three rails high, and a log cabin was erected upon it. This much they accomplished without being molested. But unfortunately for the brilliant prospects of the company, who, no doubt, expected to realize a splendid fortune from the sale of their claim, the rails of their inclosure disappeared in a most mysterious manner; the boundaries soon became extremely indefinite; every feature of its identity was lost; and at this day it is divided into more pieces than there are states in the union, furnishing fuel and timber to a large community in its vicinity. The land south of the old Indian boundary line came into market in 1835. Nearly all of it was bought by speculators, some bidding for it as high as ten and fifteen dollars per acre. In this way the settlers, in many cases, were dispossessed of their claims, including all their improvements, which had cost them years of labor. Unable to compete with the speculators, it was impossible for them to retain their lands. In view of the hardships of such cases, and for the purpose of settling lines, and making an *express* agreement with each other to carry out the *implied* agreement before alluded to, the settlers at the Big Wood formed a society, in 1836, called "The Claim Protecting Society."

It had for its object, beside the protection of the settlers against speculators, the settlement of all disputes as to boundaries. It was provided that settlers whose boundaries were fixed beyond all dispute, should measure and plat their claims, and file the same with the secretary. The other members were then bound to protect and defend them. The following preamble and resolutions are taken from the records of the Big Woods Claim Society, which was the first society of the kind formed in this county:

EAST SIDE OF THE BIG WOODS, }
Cook county, Illinois, Feb. 6, 1836.}

BE IT REMEMBERED, That we, the undersigned, inhabitants of the east side of the Big Woods and its vicinity, have settled on lands belonging to the United States, and who have severally made their respective claims, including timber and prairie: Now, for the peace and tranquility of our said settlement, we do severally and individually bind each to the other, in the penal sum of one thousand dollars, to protect and assist each other in their respective claims, and to assist each other in keeping off all intruders that may intrude on each other's claims, in any way whatever. And we further agree to deed and redeed to each other, at government price, whenever our said claims shall come into market; that is to say, in case our respective claims shall not agree or correspond with the general government survey. The true intent and meaning of these presents is, that we severally and individually shall have our lands according to our said claims that we now have claimed, whether our claims shall correspond with the actual survey or not. In case any difficulty should hereafter arise respecting any of our said claims, in any way whatever, we do severally and individually agree to let all disputes and difficulties be submitted to the following named persons, as a committee, who shall, or a majority of them, and their successors in office, settle all kinds of disputes or difficulties that may arise respecting claims whatever. The following persons were duly appointed as said committee:

DOCT. LEVI WARD,   FREDERICK STOLP,
A. E. CARPENTER,   WILLIAM J. STRONG,
        CHARLES SIDDERS.

N. B. All claims, as respecting their size, both in timber and prarie, shall be submitted to the said committee, for them to say whether any of our said claims are unreasonable in size or not. In case of any intrusion that may hereafter arise with any of our said claims, we do severally and individually agree to pay our equal quota of expenses that may arise in defense of our claims, according to the size and nature of our claims.

The above meeting was held at the house of A. Culver, on the east side of the Big Woods. JOHN WARNE, Secretary.

The following is a list of the members of this society:

John Warne,
A. E. Carpenter,
James Dyer,
John Mosier,
Joseph Fish,
J. M. Warren,
John Maxwell,
Cornelius Jones,
John Ogden,
Phineas Graves,
Wm. Hall,
David Crane,
James Brown,
Frederick Stolp,
Nelson Murray,
Taylor S. Warne,
Jesse B. Ketchum,
Barton Eddy,
David McKee,
J. S. P. Lord,
Joseph Wilson,
Warren Smith,
Henry M. Waite,
Lyman King,
Luther Chandler,
Gilbert S. Rouse,
S. H. Arnold,
Joseph Stolp,
Reuben Austin,
Charles Arnold,
Levi Leach.

Elihu Wright,
Nazah Beardsley,
S. Hurlbut,
Darias J. Lamphear,
Walter Germain,
John B. Eddy,
John Gregg,
Samuel Mosier,
Orrin W. Graves,
B. Tubbs, Jr.,
Joseph Thayer,
Thomson Paxton,
L. Ward,
Charles Brown,
Charles Sidders,
James Hymes,
Nathan Williams,
Wm. J. Strong,
Robert Hopkins,
Jesse Graves,
John Stolp,
Allen Williams,
A. Culver,
Thomas N. Paxton,
Dennis Clark,
Amander P. Thomas,
Alfred Churchill,
R. S. Ostrander,
A. W. Beardsley,
George Laird,

George C. Howes,
Samuel Paxton,
William Williams,
George Monroe,
Harvey Higbee,
N. H. Thomas,
Enos Coleman,
Linus L. Coleman,
Eli Northum,
Zerah Jones,
Reuben Jones,
George S. Blackman,
Blackman & Winslow,
William E. Bent,
J. B. & E. Smith,
Ira Woodman,
Alden S. Clifford,
Wm. Hill,
John Fox,
Nathan Williams,
Alanson Arnold,
Eleazer Blackman,
Aurin Ralph,
John Sidders,
Russel Whipple,
Sheffield Mills,
Jonas Lamphear,
Wm. R. Currier,
Manus Griswold,
Isaac Barnes,

We insert below the record of some of the transactions of this body, and also several decisions relating to disputed claims:

At a meeting this 6th day of August, A. D. 1836, at the house of Thomson Paxton, on the east side of the Big Woods, Cook county:

It was motioned and seconded that this be our first annual meeting, and our next annual meeting be held on the 6th of August next, at 1 o'clock, P. M., and to have a regular meeting every six months, or semi-annual meeting. It was motioned and seconded that the following named persons be a new committee, and they were duly elected, as follows: WILLIAM J. STRONG, THOMSON PAXTON, JOHN GREGG, WARREN SMITH, FREDERICK STOLP.

It was motioned and seconded that this society be called the BIG WOODS CLAIM PROTECTING SOCIETY. It was motioned and seconded that, at our semi-annual or annual meetings, in all cases a majority present shall have full power to do business; and further, that this instrument shall not be altered, in any case, except at the annual or semi-annual meetings.

It was further motioned and seconded, that we bind our heirs and assigns. It was motioned and seconded that the secretary purchase a book to register our respective claims; and further, it was motioned and seconded that every person shall present or give a description of his or her claim, within ninety days from this date, to the secretary, to have our respective claims recorded in a book for that purpose. Any claimant not complying as above, such claim by us shall be considered null and void. It was motioned and seconded that in all cases where any suit or suits are investigated by the committee, the defaulter or trespasser shall pay all costs. It was motioned and seconded that the penal sum of this, our said constitution, shall be increased from one to ten thousand dollars.

Motioned and seconded that this meeting adjourn to the first Saturday in February next, at 10 o'clock, A. M., to the house of Thomson Paxton.

At a meeting held this 4th day of February, 1837, at the house of Thomson Paxton, on the east side of the Big Woods, Cook county, Illinois:-

Voted, That the time be extended for entering claims, until the next annual meeting; that the descriptions handed in since the time expired should be received also, for recording. Voted, That no one settler shall be protected by this society on a claim to exceed six hundred and forty acres.

Voted, That the secretary drop a line to those individuals that have recorded more land than this society will protect them in.

Voted, That no member of our society shall commence a suit at the expense of the society, without the approbation of the committee.

Voted, That a written notice from one of the committee shall be given to the defendant, or to his wife, previous to any suit pending before them.

Voted, That our whole proceedings, from the commencement, shall be published in the three Chicago newspapers, and likewise in the Milwaukee *Advocate;* that a committee of three be appointed to draft or prepare our proceedings for publication. The following named persons were elected said committee: RUSSELL WHIPPLE, ELI NORTHAM, WARREN SMITH, including the secretary.

Voted, That the secretary shall record all decisions made by the committee respecting claims.

Voted, That this meeting adjourn to the 6th day of August next, to meet at the house of Thomson Paxton.

DECISIONS OF THE CLAIM COMMITTEE.

We, the subscribers, have taken into consideration the right of claim in dispute between J. Warren and J. Maxwell, and award that the 160 acres shall be equally divided between said claimants.

L. WARD,
CHARLES SIDERS,
F. STOLP,
WM. J. STRONG, } Committee.

Cook county, Illinois,}
  5th March, 1836. }

It was the decision of the committee that Mr. Warren has shown a right to the east eighty, by an agreement, and that Mr. Warren, therefore, has nothing more to leave out with regard to the above named lot.

WARREN SMITH,
THOMSON PAXTON,
JOHN GREGG,
F. STOLP, } Committee.

Jan. 17, 1837.

The committee agreed that the disputed quarter section within the furrow between Williams and Himes, should be equally divided between said Williams and Himes, the division line to run with the road. Williams shall take the north half and Himes the south.

Entered Feb. 4, 1837.

We, the committee of the "BIG WOODS CLAIM PROTECTING SOCIETY," give judgment on the case wherein James Dyer is plaintiff and David McKee defendant, on a lot of prairie east of David McKee's field. That the said David McKee pay the said James Dyer one hundred dollars, and have all the improvements made by the said Dyer; otherwise, if the said David McKee refuse to pay the above mentioned sum to the said Dyer, he shall have the said lot of land as his lawful claim, to dispose of as his.

A society was formed for similar objects in 1839, called the "Du Page County Society for Mutual Protection." At the risk of tiring our readers, we give some extracts from its records:

At a meeting of the settlers of DU PAGE County, held at Naperville, on the 28th of October, A. D. 1839, Russel Whipple was called to the chair, and James C. Hatch appointed secretary. Whereupon the following report was read to the meeting: At a meeting of the settlers of DU PAGE County, held at Naperville, on the 29th of September last, to take measures for securing their rights and interests to and in their respective claims, a committee of ten was appointed to draft rules and regulations to present for the consideration of this meeting, in compliance with which, said committee respectfully beg leave to present the following:

Situated as we are upon government lands, which have, by the industry of the settlers, already become highly valuable, and inasmuch as our claims lie in such a variety of shapes, and are of such different dimensions, that they cannot in any manner correspond with the government survey, it appears necessary, in order to prevent the most fearful consequences, that the lines of our respective claims should be established previous to the government survey, and we ourselves bound by the strong arm of the law, to reconvey, as hereinafter mentioned, to our neighbors, whenever these lands are sold by the order of the general government, so as to keep our claims as they are now established; and to accomplish this end, we recommend the following regulations:

First. We do hereby form ourselves into a society, to be called the DU PAGE COUNTY SOCIETY FOR MUTUAL PROTECTION, and agree to be governed by such prudent rules and by-laws as the society may hereafter adopt, not inconsistent with the laws of the country; and that we will make use of all honorable means to protect each other in our respective claims, as may hereafter be agreed upon and recorded; and that we will not countenance any unjust claim, set up by speculators or others; and we declare that the primary object of this society is, to protect the inhabitants in their claims and boundaries, so that each shall deed and redeed to the other as hereinafter mentioned, when the government survey does not agree with the present lines, or lines which may hereafter be agreed upon.

Second. That there be a committee of five appointed at this meeting, three of whom may form a board of arbitration, to decide, from legal testimony, all disputes respecting the lines or boundaries of any claim to which they may be called together, with the costs of the arbitration, and the party or parties who shall pay the same: *Provided,* It does not appear that such dispute has previously been decided, by an arbitration held by the agreement of the parties, which shall be a bar against further proceedings of said committee, except as to matter of costs.

Third. That each of the said committee shall be entitled to one dollar per day, for each day officially engaged.

Fourth. That, in all cases where the parties cannot establish their lines, either by reference to their neighbors or otherwise, either party may, at any time, by giving to the other ten days' notice of his or her intention, call out at least three of the board of arbitration, to decide the same, and their decision shall be final.

Fifth. That there be one clerk appointed at this meeting, who shall keep a fair record of all transactions of this association, and also of all descriptions of claims presented to him for record: *Provided,* That there is attached thereto a certificate from all who have adjoining claims, certifying to the correctness of such description, or a certificate signed by a majority of any arbitration, met to establish any line or lines of said claim; and that the said clerk shall be entitled to twenty-five cents for recording each claim and certificate.

Sixth. That it shall be the duty of every settler to present to the clerk a definite description of his or her claim, either from actual survey or otherwise, and also to set his or her hand and seal to a certain indenture, drafted by Giles Spring, Esq., of Chicago, for this society.

Seventh. That there be a committee of three in each precinct, appointed at this meeting, for the purpose of carrying into effect the sixth regulation.

Eighth. That the settlers on the school lands ought to obtain their lands at government price.

Ninth. That we will firmly and manfully protect all who conform to the above regulations previous to the first day of January, 1840.

Which report and regulations were unanimously adopted, and ordered to be embodied in a constitution.

Thereafter, on motion, a committee of six was appointed by the chair, to nominate a board of arbitration and clerk, viz.: Lewis Ellsworth, Elihu Thayer, Luther Hatch, Cornelius Jones, Job A. Smith, and David S. Dunning; who, having retired, returned and reported LYMAN MEACHAM, ERASTUS GARY, and STEPHEN J. SCOTT, board of arbitration, and P. BALLINGALL, clerk; which nominations were approved of.

Whereupon, it was moved and adopted, that the following persons be the precinct committees, viz. :

NAPERVILLE PRECINCT.—Stephen J. Scott, Henry Goodrich, Nathan Allen, Jr.

WEBSTER PRECINCT.—John W. Walker, James C. Hatch, Pierce Downer.

DEERFIELD PRECINCT.—Luther Morton, Perus Barney, Moses Stacy.

WASHINGTON PRECINCT.—Lyman Meacham, Smith D. Pierce, Capt. E. Kinny.

ORANGE PRECINCT.—Job A. Smith, Wm. Kimball, Luther F. Sanderson.

DU PAGE PRECINCT.—Warren Smith, Lorin G. Hulbert, Alvah Fowler.

BIG WOODS PRECINCT.—John Warne, Levi Leach, William J. Strong.

Resolved, That this meeting adjourn till the first Monday in January, 1840.

                          RUSSELL WHIPPLE, Chairman.
JAS. C. HATCH, Secretary.

At a meeting of the "Du Page County Society for Mutual Protection," held at Naperville, the sixth day of January, A. D. 1840, in pursuance of adjournment, Russell Whipple took the chair, when, on motion of Mr. Geo. Martin, it was

Resolved, That the time for recording the claims of the members of this society, in order to secure the benefits of the ninth resolution of the meeting held on the 28th of October last, be extended till the first day of march next.

On motion of Mr. James C. Hatch,

Resolved, That the claims belonging to members of the society which lie on the line of, or in another county, shall be entitled to record and protection, on the member complying with the fifth regulation.

On motion of Mr. Lyman Meacham,

Resolved, That when a claim belonging to a member of this association shall border on that of a non-resident, or that of a person out of the state, or on land not occupied, the same shall be recorded if a certificate from the adjoining claimants be attached thereto, certifying to such non-residence, absence, or non-occupancy, and that there is no dispute concerning the same.

On motion of Mr. William J. Strong,

Resolved, That any member of this society who, in an arbitration, fails to establish his claim before the board of arbitration, shall pay the costs thereof within six days from the decision being pronounced, and failing to make such payment, he shall cease to be a member of this society.

Resolved, That this meeting adjourn until the first Monday in March next.   P. BALLINGALL, *Clerk.*

At a meeting of the society, held at Naperville, on the 6th day of January, A. D. 1840, in pursuance of adjournment, Stephen J. Scott was appointed chairman.

Resolved, That James Johnson and Isaac B. Berry be allowed another trial in their arbitration with Harry T. Wilson, on condition that said Johnson and Berry pay one counsel fee, and the whole costs of the arbitration.

Resolved, That the board of arbitrators shall have power to fill all vacancies occasioned by death, removal, or otherwise, between this time and the first Monday in May next.

Resolved, That the resolution offered by William J. Strong, and passed at last meeting, be and is hereby repealed.

Resolved, That the line between Ephraim Collar and Timothy E. Parsons is hereby declared to be the road leading from —— to ——, laid by Butterfield, Church and Arnold, as the same has been recorded.

Resolved, That this meeting adjourn till the first Monday in May next.

P. BALLINGALL, *Clerk.*

3

At a meeting of the Du Page County Society for Mutual Protection, held at Naperville, on Monday, the 4th day of May, A. D. 1840, pursuant to adjournment, John Stevens was appointed chairman, and James F. Wight clerk, *pro tem.*, when, on motion of Mr. P. Downer,

Resolved, That the time for settling and recording claims of the members of this society be extended to the first Monday in June next.

Resolved, That this meeting adjourn until the first Monday in June next, then to meet in Naperville.

J. F. WIGHT, *Clerk, pro tem.*

At a meeting of the Du Page County Society for Mutual Protection, held at Naperville, on Monday, the 1st day (being the first Monday) in June, 1840, pursuant to adjournment, Captain John Stevens was appointed chairman. Patrick Ballingall, Esq., having resigned the office of clerk of this society, on motion of Mr. Hunt,

Resolved, That James F. Wight be and is hereby appointed clerk of this society, in the place of P. Ballingall, Esq., resigned.

Resolved, That the time for settling and recording claims of the members of this society be extended until the first Monday in September next. On motion of Mr. James C. Hatch,

Resolved, That the Clerk hereafter record no certificates of claims unless it is certified that they are the only claimants adjoining the claim or claims offered to be recorded, or for want of such certificate, that the applicant shall make oath that no other person except those named in such certificate adjoin him.

Resolved, That the clerk notify all persons whose claims are recorded (without their having signed the settler's bond), that they sign the said bond, or they will not be protected by this society.

Resolved, That this meeting adjourn to the first Monday in September next, then to meet at the Preëmption House, in Naperville, at one o'clock, P. M.

JAMES F. WIGHT, *Clerk.*

At a meeting of the Du Page County Society for Mutual Protection, held at Naperville, on Wednesday, the 3d day of March, 1841, Hon. Russell Whipple was called to the chair, and Morris Sleight appointed Secretary. After the object of the meeting had been stated by Stephen J. Scott, the following persons were appointed a committee to draft resolutions expressive of the sense of this meeting, viz.: LUTHER HATCH, STEPHEN J. SCOTT, WILLIAM J. STRONG, and ISAAC CLARK.

On motion of N. Allen, jr., Esq., Aylmer Keith was appointed clerk of this society, to record claims and the certificates for the same, and to keep the settlers' book, in place of James F. Wight.

Resolved, That the time for recording claims be extended to the first Monday of September, 1841.

The committee appointed to draft resolutions reported the following, which were adopted, with one or two dissenting votes:

Whereas, It is generally believed that the public lands on which we hold settlers' claims will be shortly offered for sale, and in order that each claimant may obtain and feel secure in the possession of his just claim, it is deemed necessary that there be a uniformity of action and feeling on the subject, and believing that the proving up of preëmption claims will have a tendency to create excitement and confusion, if not to interfere with the rights of others: Therefore be it

Resolved, 1. That we will not prove up our preëmption claims, even when justly entitled to do so, except in cases where it may be deemed necessary to secure the claimant, but that we will not do so without the consent of a committee to be appointed by this union, or the several towns, to settle disputes.

Resolved, 2. That any person who shall attempt to obtain a preëmption, and thereby seize upon any part of any other person's claim, shall be deemed a dishonest man, not entitled to the protection of this union, and shall not be allowed to purchase any other land in this county, if this union can prevent it.

Resolved, 3. That when the inhabitants of any township shall guarantee to those on the school section, and entitled to a float, that they shall have their claim at ten shillings per acre; then, in such case, if they shall obtain, or attempt to obtain a float, or lay one upon any other claimant's just claim, they shall be considered no better than a thief or a robber, and shall have no protection from this union.

Resolved, 4. That it is the duty of this association to take measures to secure to claimants on the school section their claims at government price.

Resolved, 5. That the protection of this union will not be extended to any person who shall either take or purchase a school section float, except the township refuse to guarantee, as in the third resolution.

Resolved, 6. That the several townships in this county call meetings and make such arrangements, and adopt such measures as may be thought necessary, with regard to their claims at the approaching land sale.

Resolved, 7. That the proceedings of this meeting be forwarded by the secretary to the land office in Chicago, and ask of the register and

.receiver to act with regard to lands in this county on the spirit of the resolutions here passed.

Resolved, 8. That the proceedings of this meeting be signed by the chairman and secretary, and published in the Chicago papers.

Subordinate claim societies were organized in each of the precincts of the county; the settlers pretty generally joined them, and many difficulties were adjusted by this means among the squatters. The hard times which followed the crisis of 1836 and 1837, discouraged speculation somewhat, and but few were able to purchase the land which they had improved, and some were unable to do that. The pledges made by the members of the claim societies were uniformly carried out, and all honorable men gave no cause of complaint to their neighbors. In a few cases some less scrupulous refused to deed lands in their possession to the rightful owner, and in consequence quarrels and some suits at law were the result. Some of these suits are still " pending and undecided."

We subjoin a few instances, showing how summarily a certain class of claim difficulties were disposed of. Many more might be added, but let these suffice.

Two neighbors owned adjoining claims, and at the time of the organization of the claim society their land was being surveyed by the government surveyor. One of the men happened to be a member of the society, and the other not. It so happened that the random line, run by the surveyor, cut off a portion of the claim of the first, and left it in such a manner that the other would be entitled to a preëmption upon it. When he discovered this, he refused to deed the land to the one who claimed it. Persuasion was used in vain. He thought he had the advantage of his neighbor, and determined to keep it. In a few days, however, matters assumed a different light, and then the line was established so as to give back to the society man not only what he claimed, but also a large corner from his neighbor's tract, and now *he* was entitled to a preëmption. The obstinate man was thus induced to join the society, and take upon himself the obligation to "deed and re-deed." After being kept in suspense for a while, by way of punishment, his land was again restored to him.

There were many of the settlers who did not join the claim societies, but among all *bona-fide* settlers there prevailed a determination to protect each other. The first trouble arising from "claim jumping," was in 1836, or thereabouts, respecting the claim of Mr. Frothingham, in the town of Milton. A family of squatters came on and took possession of a portion of his claim, without leave or license, and were determined to remain there in spite of entreaty or physical force. The settlement was apprised of this state of affairs, and a company of about fifty horsemen proceeded to the cabin of the incorrigible squatters, who, on seeing them coming, broke for tall timber, leaving but one occupant in the cabin, an old lady who had passed the running point. The sum of seventeen dollars was raised among the company to indemnify the family for sundry outlays which they had made upon the premises. This the old lady received upon condition that the family should quit the claim without delay. To expedite the execution of her part of the contract, the settlers fell to work and assisted in the removal of the furniture from the house, and in clearing the premises of everything that belonged to the family. After this had been done, the house was torn down and the rubbish thrown into a heap near by, preparatory to kindling a bonfire, when the "meeting" was called to order and several stump speeches of a decidedly inflammatory character were made. We are not in possession of the minutes of those speeches, but have been informed that the Hon. Nathan Allen figured quite conspicuously in this part of the exercises. His speech on that occasion is spoken of as being one of his most felicitous and pointed "efforts." When the speech-making had subsided, fire was set to the heap of promiscuous ruins, and the hut of the interlopers was soon reduced to ruins. The conduct of the settlers in this case proved a warning to future intruders, and claim jumping was rarely heard of in that part of the county afterward.

A man from Plumb Grove happened to be on his way to the Naper settlement and passing near the place while the affair just described was taking place. Seeing the smoke ascend from the spot, and hearing the universal uproar among the settlers, he concluded at once that a party of Indians was there, killing and laying waste. Turning from the beaten track which led near the house, he made a circuit around the "marauders," and lashing his horses to their utmost speed, rode to the settlement, warning everybody to flee for their lives. The cause of his fright was pretty generally understood, and therefore he did not succeed in getting up a very serious alarm.

A few years after a contention arose respecting the

Tullis claim, which was situated in the same neighborhood. Under a preëmption law passed about that time, a man by the name of Harmond undertook to preëmpt a portion of the claim of Mr. Tullis, who had already obtained possession of it under a former preëmption act. In order to comply with the provisions of the later act, Harmond built a *pen* of small poles near the center of his claim, staid in it only one night, and started immediately for Chicago to prove his preëmption. On his return, he commenced making repairs upon an old block house which was already built upon his " quarter," and being asked why he was doing it, replied that he had preëmpted that claim, and was going to live there. This aroused the indignation of the neighboring squatters, who called a meeting to take into consideration the conduct of Mr. Harmond. He, being present, was advised to relinquish his claim, but he positively refused to do it, and at the same time threw out some pretty savage threats against the settlers, in case they attempted to remove him by force. After a long consultation, it was concluded that the building on the premises should be torn down if he did not abandon it without delay. At this decision Harmond became greatly exasperated, and having his rifle with him, threatened to fire upon " the first man who should tear off a board." Whereupon a fearless Qaker gentleman stepped forth and remarked to Mr. Harmond that if he designed to put that threat in execution he had better begin by shooting at *him*, as he considered himself a mark of sufficient magnitude for a *claim jumper* to shoot at, any how. The old Quaker was soon joined by Lyman Butterfield,

who addressed Mr. Harmond in pretty much the same
strain, informing him that if he was not willing to waste
his powder on one man, he would offer the additional
inducement of placing his own body in fair range, so
that he might at least kill "*two* birds with one stone."
But Harmond could not be prevailed upon to shoot,
and so the party proceeded to the disputed claim,
tearing down the house, and removing every vestige
of former occupancy. Before ten minutes had elapsed,
after the decision of the council of settlers, this was
done, and Mr. Harmond was sent on his way to other
parts, not rejoicing, but uttering the most awful denunciations against such ungentlemanly treatment.

In justice to a numerous class of our early settlers,
we deem it appropriate to introduce here a brief notice
of a society which was formed in 1834, and known as
the " Hognatorial Council." We have ransacked all
the dead languages we ever heard of, in order to obtain
for our readers some clue to the origin of this *preno-
men*, but have been signally defeated in the undertaking. Its origin is altogether too obscure for us, and we
leave the task of tracing it to more able and willing
hands. The object of the ".council" seems to have
been the settling of a peculiar class of claim difficulties,
which were not taken cognizance of by the *bona fide*
claim committee, and its operations were designed to
burlesque the proceedings of that committee, as well
as to ridicule courts in general. All disputes brought
before the " Hognatorial " were settled in a summary
and satisfactory manner. We can illustrate this remark
with but one instance, which occurred in the south
part of the county. A man by the name of Clarke,

who was firmly grounded in Midshipman Easy's doctrine of "what belongs to my neighbor belongs also to me," made a "claim" upon another man's land, lying somewhere on the Du Page river. Finding that peaceable and quiet possession was impossible, he applied to a gentleman who happened to be posted in "hognatorial" matters, for advice. He was of course advised to bring the matter before the "Hognatorial Council," as that was the only reliable tribunal having jurisdiction over such grievances. His case was prepared by Nathan Allen, a man of superior legal attainments, and upon a certain day the Hognatorial Council room was crowded to witness the proceedings in the case. Allen opened the case by giving to the jury a plain unvarnished statement of the facts, and closed it by a most pathetic appeal to their sense of justice, in behalf of his wronged and injured client. Several witnesses were called upon to testify, and the upshot of the testimony was that Mr. Clark had a claim commencing at a certain point on Du Page river, but in what direction his lines ran from that point it was impossible to ascertain. Several hours were occupied in examining witnesses, during which time Clark kept a boy running to and fro between the "council chamber" and his house, to inform his wife of the different phases which the case assumed as the trial progressed. At length the testimony was all in, the closing argument made, and the case submitted to the jury. There was but one point left for the jury to act upon, and that related particularly to the boundary of Clark's claim. They were out but a short time, and returned the following verdict: "We, the

*3

jurors in this case, decide that Mr. Clark is justly
entitled to a piece of land lying on the Du Page river,
and described as follows, to wit: commencing at a
certain point on the east bank of said river, and running perpendicular to the horizon *straight up*." This
was enough for Clark. He hastened to communicate
the result to his waiting, anxious wife, and afterward
proceeded to the tavern and got ingloriously drunk
over the result of his victorious suit.

GENERAL VIEW OF THE COUNTY.

SITUATION, EXTENT, ETC.

THE County of DU PAGE, is situated in the northern part of the State of Illinois, and consists of a fraction over nine townships. It belonged originally to Cook county, until its separation and organization into a distinct county by act of Legislature, passed at the session of 1839. It is bounded on the north and east by Cook county, on the south by Will and Cook, and on the west by Kane.

The early settlers were almost wholly of English extraction, but the population of the present day consists of a mixture of English and Germans. The following table will show when the several towns were organized, when first settled and by whom, and also the number of inhabitants, according to the census of 1850 and 1855:

TOWNS.	SETTLED.	BY WHOM.	ORGANIZED.	NO. INHABITANTS.	
				1850	1855
Addison, ...	1834	H. Duncklee,......	1850	812	1,262
Bloomingdale,..........	1833	S.L. & H. Meacham	1850	897	1,214
Downer's Grove,........	1833	Wells & Grant,....	1850	959	1,015
Lisle,.................	1830	Baley Hobson,....	1850	1,137	1,466
Milton,.	1831	H. T. Wilson, ...	1850	1,005	1,841
Naperville,...........	1831	Joseph Naper,....	1850	1,628	2,055
Winfield,.............	1832	E. & J. P. Gary,...	1850	1,149	1,533
Wayne, ...	1834	John Laughlin,....	1850	855	1,039
York, ...	1834	Elisha Fish,.......	1850	853	1,842
				9,299	12,807

The number of inhabitants to the square mile, omitting fractions, was in 1850, twenty-two, in 1855, twenty-nine.

The following items are taken from the census of 1855. There are fifty-two manufactories, of all kinds, in the county, and the value of manufactured products, is $161,095. The value of live stock is $876,185. There were 104,761 pounds of wool produced. There were seventy-two common schools taught in the county, being an increase of twenty over the preceding census. There were three academies; number of pupils, 5,770. The population included *one negro*, and one Indian.

FACE OF THE COUNTRY, ETC.

Du Page County is generally level, and contains fair proportions of timber and prairie. The soil is well adapted to grazing, and produces abundant crops of all kinds of grain common to this latitude. The Du Page river, which has its rise in the northern part of the county, is skirted with forests of thrifty growing timber. In addition to the facilities thus afforded for timber and fuel, the inhabitants in the western part have recourse to the Big Woods, which lie partly in this county. The west branch of the Du Page, is a stream of considerable size, and affords numerous sites for the application of water power. Besides several saw mills, and other manufactories, there are flouring mills situated upon this stream, at Warrenville, Naperville, and at Hobson's.

There are no other streams of much importance in the county, yet it is well watered by the smaller streams and springs, which are everywhere to be found. The average depth of wells is about twenty-five feet.

PRODUCTS OF CULTIVATION.

The chief staples are corn, wheat, rye, oats, and potatoes; but barley, buckwheat, peas and beans, are cultivated to some extent. Considerable attention is given to fruit raising. Orchards are generally young, and the adaptation of this climate to the culture of the apple, has not been fully tested. The prospect, however, for a productive season, has never been so encouraging as at present. The productions of horticulture, are chiefly of the most common and useful kinds. Rare and delicate plants are to be found in few gardens. The grape is cultivated to considerable extent, and produces abundantly. Locust trees abound. The horse chestnut, larch, mountain ash, and various other species of the ornamental class, are generally introduced. The forests furnish a good variety of shade trees. Of the sugar maple, elm, ash, butternut, and soft maple, large quantities are transplanted to the farms and villages, every season. These will eventually take the place of the locust, which proves too susceptible to the severity of our winters, many having died out during the past two years. Du Page is ranked as an agricultural county, but the attention of farmers has been directed to the raising of cattle, and it is thought by many, that the production of grain will gradually give place to the increase and improvement of stock.

The "Du Page County Agricultural and Mechanical Society," was formed in 1854. Its design is to

promote a friendly intercourse among the citizens, as
well as improvement and enterprise in the cultivation
of the soil, raising of stock, and the manufacture of
useful farming and household utensils. The annual
fair of this society is held about the middle of September. The place of meeting is now fixed at Wheaton,
the society having secured at that place twenty acres of
valuable land, fifteen acres of which were donated by
J. C. and W. L. Wheaton. The operations of this
society, it is believed, are attended with many important results. It calls the attention of the farming
community to the better management of their farms;
to the greater production and more beneficial employment of manures; to the introduction of choice breeds
of live stock, of all kinds, and especially working
cattle, horses, cows, and sheep. By its annual premi-
ums it excites emulation, and promotes a spirit of
enterprise and activity among the agriculturists. By
the same means, it awakens kindred feelings among
the women, and improves various and important
articles of domestic manufacture. The farmers are
generally the owners of the soil; they form a body of
yeomanry deeply interested in the improvement of
their farms, and the industrious habits of citizens—one
of the grand supports of our free and happy government. Success then to this society, and may each
succeeding year mark its nearer approach to the
worthy object for which it was formed.

EDUCATION, SCHOOLS AND ACADEMIES.

The more judicious laws of recent times, have done
much for the interest of our schools. These laws have

been well observed by the people of DU PAGE County. We now have about seventy school districts, which are provided with good school buildings and good schools. Much of our advancement in this respect, is due to the indefatigable labors of our late school commissioner, Rev. Hope Brown. From Mr. Brown's annual report of 1855, we give some extracts showing the state of our schools at that time :

"The whole number of school districts in the county is sixty-eight, sixty-four of which are provided with school houses. If we divide these houses into four classes, we may reckon twenty in the first class, and call them *extra;* we may also reckon twenty in the second class, and call them *good;* we may reckon sixteen in the third class, and call them *passable;* and that will leave eight for the fourth class, which may justly be called MISERABLE. Three new houses have been erected the last year, and preparations are being made for the erection of several more the present year. In relation to this subject, there is generally, throughout the county, a disposition to make progress in the right direction. No district is willing to have its school house reported year after year, as being miserably poor, and entirely unfit to be occupied for school purposes. Since I first began to visit our schools, five years ago, and to report the condition of the school houses in our county paper, thirty new ones have been erected, and several others have undergone important repairs; and the prospect now is, that no district will be long without a house that they will be unwilling to have visited and reported *just as it is.* The whole number of pupils connected with our district schools the past winter, is not far from two thousand; among this number, about twelve hundred have attended to arithmetic, five hundred have studied geography, two hundred and fifty English grammar, and about one hundred have attended to higher branches, such as algebra, natural philosophy, physiology, and the history of the United States.

"The schools have generally been taught from six to eight months each, during the year. In a few districts there has been no school during the winter. The wages of teachers have been, for females, from eight to sixteen dollars per month and board; for males, from sixteen to thirty per month and board. It is an omen of good, that there is a disposition to give to teachers a better remuneration for their services, than they have received in years past. When good wages are offered, then good qualifications may be rigidly insisted upon. Of all cheap things, cheap teachers are the first to be repudiated. When, by the special pleading of school directors, I am urged to give a certificate to a teacher, whom I have good reason to regard as unqualified to instruct in each of the branches required by law to be taught in our district schools, I feel that I am asked to do that which will not be likely to promote the interests of education in any school. The district that cannot afford to have a good teacher, should not throw away their money by employing a poor teacher. In examining teachers, I may have been regarded as being unnecessarily strict, but I have at all times aimed to be governed by "law and evidence," and where I have refused a certificate, it has been because the applicant has not furnished evidence on examination, that he possessed the qualifications which the law requires. If, in respect to this important duty I have erred, it has been in being too lenient rather than in being too strict. If none but those who are well qualified, as the law requires, can be approbated, then none but such as regard themselves as well qualified, will be likely to apply for or consent to be employed in any school in our county. In visiting and examining our schools the past winter, I found them generally in a prosperous condition. To this general remark there may be three or four exceptions; and where these exceptions apply, if school directors had been faithful in the discharge of the duties devolving upon them as such, these schools would no doubt have been much better than what they were. As a whole, our district schools may be regarded as doing much, very much, for the advancement of the prosperity of our county.

"In addition to our district schools, there are in the county three incorporated academies, 'The Naperville Academy,' 'The Illinois Institute' and the 'Warrenville Seminary;' the two former of which are in a prosperous condition, but the latter is suspended for the present. There are also six private schools in the county. In these schools and in the above named academies, there have been the past winter, about five hundred pupils; so that in view of our academies and schools, public and private, we may regard this county as well furnished with the means of education, or at least in a fair way to be well furnished. Let the same progress in respect to schools be made in this county for five years to come, which has been made during the preceding five years, and but few counties, either west or east, will be better furnished with the means of education than will Du Page County. School directors, in many instances, have been sadly delinquent in relation to the duty of visiting schools under their immediate supervision. It is believed that there are those who sustain this responsible office, who have not visited the schools legally under their care, even once during the entire year. Such do not magnify their office, nor does their office magnify them. But a word to the wise may be sufficient."

A brief notice of our incorporated institutions of learning will be found in the histories of the towns in which they are situated.

HEALTH.

This county is proverbial for its healthfulness, but diseases of the more acute form, as billious and typhus fevers, fever and ague, are not uncommon at some seasons of the year. The climate is mild and salubrious. The heat of the summer is perhaps greater than it is in the same latitude of the eastern states, but our winters are far less severe.

THE COUNTY PRESS.

To write out the newspaper history of Du Page County, is but to record a succession of failures. The first newspaper was established at the county seat. Being situated on the principal route for transit between the Rock river country and Chicago, Naperville had grown to be a considerable town, and in 1849 its citizens naturally thought that an organ, or newspaper, was necessary to give it position and honorable mention among its sister towns. Accordingly, with a liberality which was characteristic, its citizens offered to purchase a printing press and materials for any one who would undertake to publish a newspaper in Naperville. Unfortunately for them, their liberal offer was heard of by an adventurer named Charles J. Sellon, who hastened to Naperville, and early in November, 1849, struck a bargain with the citizens, and agreed to publish a paper on the terms proposed. Sellon was wholly unknown to the people of Naperville, had no capital, and but little reputation, though he had but a short time previous been engaged in two or three unsuccessful and dishonorable newspaper speculations. However, the citizens were as good as their promise, and in two or three days raised the amount necessary, some $500, with which a second-hand press, a large quantity of type, which had previously been used on the Chicago JOURNAL, job type, and other necessary materials, were purchased, and brought to Naperville, amid the rejoicings of the people. A room was procured in the old Tarbox store for an office, and after considerable delay in arranging everything, and setting up the press and fixtures, the first number of the Du Page County Recorder was issued, if we mistake not, on or about the 1st of December, 1849, "by C. J. Sellon, Editor and Proprietor." The paper, in its commencement, was a decided success. It started off with a circulation of about 500. The business men of Naperville advertised largely, and furnished job work liberally. In fact, the establishment of the Recorder marked an era in the history of Du Page County; for although the town did not in consequence grow in population, as some other towns had done, yet it infused new life, new ideas, new ambition and energy into the business men, and the whole commu-

nity. But the success of the paper was doomed to be
of short duration. Sellon proved to be a bad manager,
lazy and extravagant, and the most liberal patronage
could not long keep him up; besides, he had no sta-
mina, was full of wild chimerical schemes, and
continually trying something new, most unfitting
qualities for a newspaper publisher. The RECORDER
having been started by the joint efforts of all parties,
it was deemed proper that it should be neutral in
politics. But Sellon's uneasy nature could not long
rest under this state of affairs, and his means running
low, he at last prevailed on one or two very susceptible
politicians, who lived out of the county, to furnish him
funds with which to change the RECORDER into a
political paper. Accordingly, at the end of nine
months, he discontinued the RECORDER, and issued
in its stead, the DEMOCRATIC PLAINDEALER. About
the same time also, he commenced the publication of
a small weekly sheet called the DAUGHTER OF TEM-
PERANCE, as he professed to be a great advocate of the
cause of temperance. The change in the character of
the paper gave great dissatisfaction to the men of both
parties in the town. The printing of the two papers
became very expensive, while there was a manifest
falling off in patronage, and some time in November,
1850, Sellon started off on a tour for the ostensible
purpose of obtaining subscribers for the DAUGHTER,
but he never came back, leaving $500 or $600 due
creditors, and an interesting family wholly destitute.
The whole concern, of course, came to a "dead lock,"
and the DEMOCRATIC PLAINDEALER and DAUGHTER OF
TEMPERANCE abruptly and ingloriously terminated their

existence, and were numbered among things that were, after a spasmodic existence of only three months.

Previous to leaving, Sellon had privately formed a partnership with H. S. Humphrey, a journeyman printer in his office, to whom he owed a considerable amount, in which he had agreed to sell him half the office, Humphrey turning his account in part payment. This gave Humphrey a lien or claim upon the office, and Keith and Barnes agreeing to become responsible to those of Sellon's creditors who were original subscribers, and still owned stock in the concern, for the payment of their claims, the office was again placed on a business footing, and early in January, 1851, the DU PAGE COUNTY OBSERVER, was issued under the management of Barnes, Humphrey and Keith. But the miserable failure and equivocal conduct of Sellon threw a "wet blanket" on the newspaper business of DU PAGE County, from which it has never yet recovered, and the OBSERVER never proved a money making concern.

Mr. Humphrey continued his connection with the paper until April 6th, 1852, when he disposed of his interest to Mr. Gershom Martin, who continued the paper two years more in connection with Barnes and Keith. In March, 1854, they transferred their interest to Mr. Martin, who continued it alone until the first of the following September, when he suspended its publication, having at that time less than 275 subscribers. Thus the OBSERVER, after a precarious existence of three years and eight months, expired. During the fall of 1854 Mr. Charles W. Keith, believing that a paper could be sustained in DU PAGE County, bought the office, procured a new and larger press, and in November, 1854, started the Du Page County Journal, a large and handsome sheet, and a decided improvement on the former ones. The Journal was continued successively by C. W. Keith; Keith, Edson & Co.; J. M. Edson, and E. M. Day, until the great and disastrous freshet of February, 1857, when the entire office, and the building it was in, was carried away by the flood.

Sometime in the summer of 1856, the citizens of Wheaton, a town which had grown up on the Galena railroad, believing the interests of their town demanded such an enterprise, procured a press, and commenced the publication at their place, of the Du Page County Gazette, J. A. J. Birdsall being the publisher. It was published about ten months, when it was discontinued. At present there is but one paper printed in the county. The Naperville Newsletter is published at Naperville, by E. H. Eyer. It is a very respectable sheet and bids fair to rival its predecessors in permanence and usefulness.

ORGANIZATION OF THE COUNTY, ETC.

The law organizing the county was approved February 9th, 1839. The boundaries of the county, as specified in the first section of the act, embraced not only the present limits, but the north half of two townships of Will county. The same section contained a proviso, as follows:

"That no part of the county above described, now forming a part of Will county, shall be included within the said county of Du Page, unless the inhabitants now residing in said part of Will county shall, by a vote to be given by them at the next August election, decide, by a majority of legal voters, that they prefer to have the said territory made a part of the said county of Du Page."

A vote of the inhabitants of the two half townships was had at the election mentioned in the proviso quoted, and although great exertions were made to produce a different result, the proposition was rejected by *one* vote.

By the fourth section of the act, Ralph Woodruff, of La Salle county, Seth Reed, of Kane county, and H. G. Loomis, of Cook county, were appointed commissioners to locate the county seat, and were to meet at the Preëmption House, in Naperville, on the first Monday of June, 1839, or within thirty days thereafter.

There was a proviso to the fourth section, as follows:

"The said commissioners shall obtain for the county, from the claimant, a quantity of land, not less than three acres, and three thousand dollars, for the purpose of erecting county buildings; which sum shall be secured to the county commissioners, and paid out, under their directions, for the purposes aforesaid."

Naperville was selected as the county seat, and on the 17th day of June, 1839, a quit-claim deed was executed to the county commissioners, conveying all the title one claimant had (the undivided half) to the present public square. The county never had title to the other half *as a claim*.

As there are many in our county who have erroneous ideas in regard to the title of the county to the public square, upon which the county buildings stand, we here insert so much of the records as are necessary to give a correct understanding of its situation.

By reference to the proceedings of the county commissioners, we find that on the 7th day of June, 1842, the following orders were entered on record by them, viz. :

"It is ordered by the court that Bailey Hobson be and he is hereby appointed a commissioner for the county of Du Page, to apply for, and obtain from the government of the United States of America, in pursuance of the act of congress in such case made and provided, a preëmption to the following described quarter section of land, to wit: The south-west quarter of section 18, township 38 north, range ten east of the third principal meridian, the same being the quarter section upon which the seat of justice for the county of Du Page is located."

" *Whereas*, Bailey Hobson, by an order entered on the records of this court, has been appointed a commissioner to apply for and obtain from the government of the United States, a preëmption to the south-west quarter section of section eighteen, township thirty-eight north, range ten east of the third principal meridian for the use of said county of Du Page, and there being several persons who have a just and equitable claim to a part of said quarter section, it is ordered by this court that the said Bailey Hobson, commissioner aforesaid, be, and he is hereby

authorized and empowered, for and in behalf of the said county of Du
Page, to convey, by good and sufficient deed, to all those persons, severally, who have a just and equitable claim to any part or portion of said
quarter section, the several proportions which any such individuals may
be justly entitled to, of said quarter section of land, upon condition that
such individuals who have a just claim to any portion of said land shall
pay to the said commissioner, for the use of said county, one dollar and
twenty-five cents per acre for the several proportions they are entitled
to, together with a further sum of money sufficient to cover and pay any
and every expense which the county aforesaid, through their said commissioner, may have to incur in proving a preëmption to said quarter section, and all their expenses attending the conveyance of said land from
the county to said individuals."

In compliance with the first order, a preëmption was
obtained under the Act of Congress of 1822, by Mr.
Hobson, as commissioner for the county, to the S. W¼
Sec. 18, T. 38 N., R. 10 E., and he, as such commissioner,
received a "duplicate" for the land, which is recorded
in the recorder's office, in book one, page 541.
Whether the "patent" for the land has been obtained
from the land office or not, we do not know.

In compliance with the second order of the county
commissioner, all the land entered by the commissioner, except the public square, was conveyed by
him to C. B. Hosmer and Lewis Ellsworth, the former
receiving a deed for that portion lying north of the
"Galena road," and the latter for that lying south of
the road.

We might give a further history of the "claim,"
but as it is foreign to our intentions to state anything
more than what is necessary to explain the situation
of the county property, we forbear.

About $5,000 was subscribed by the citizens of Na-
perville to erect a court house, which was built in 1839.
The brick offices were subsequently erected.

The county buildings, after a lapse of nearly twenty years, remain *in statu quo*, nothing having been done to beautify the grounds, or to improve their convenience or comfort. In view of the possibility of their removal, the citizens of Naperville filed a bond in the clerk's office, in April, 1857, which obligates them to enlarge and improve the appearance of the court house during the present summer. The citizens of the county are looking for a faithful execution of that bond. There being no correct view of the county buildings now extant, we are obliged to forego the pleasure of presenting our readers with a representation of their massive proportions. Since the erection of the county buildings, the judicial courts have been held uniformly at Naperville. In the winter of 1857, the Legislature passed an act, authorizing an election to be held on the first Monday in May, which should decide the question of the removal of the county seat to the town of Wheaton. The election excited considerable agitation and feeling, but the attempt was unsuccessful. Local jealousies have grown out of it, but it is hoped that they will now cease, and the great object be to elevate each town and the whole county. The circuit court holds its sessions semi-annually, on the second Monday in April, and the third Monday in October. The present presiding judge of this court is Hon. J. O. Norton, of Joliet. The probate court holds its sessions on the first Monday in each month. The present judge of probate is Walter Blanchard, of Downer's Grove. The amount of litigation carried on in this county is very small in proportion to the population. The sessions of the circuit court seldom last more than

4

two or three days. There has been but one execution
in this county for capital offense. Patrick Doyle, a
native of Ireland, was hung at Naperville, in 1854,
for the murder of Patrick Tole.

The following account of this murder is taken from
the Du PAGE OBSERVER, of October 26, 1853:

"On Monday of last week a most revolting murder
was committed on the line of the Chicago, St. Charles
and Mississippi Air Line Railroad, in this county.
The particulars, so far as we have been able to learn
them, are about as follows: Two brothers, Irishmen,
named Tole, who had been employed upon the road,
had received their pay in the morning, amounting to
sixty dollars, and had quit work. They were indulging
in a little 'spree,' and one of them became very drunk.
An Irishman named Doyle, by some means was knowing to the fact of their having the money in their
possession, and it is supposed determined upon robbing
them. He found an opportunity to make the attempt
the same afternoon. It seems all three were traveling
along together on the St. Charles and Chicago wagon
road, and when near the residence of Mr. Clisby, one
of the brothers Tole became so stupid from the effects
of liquor as to be unable to proceed further; in other
words, he was dead drunk, and fell down in the fence
corner. The sober brother stopped to move him, and
assist him to proceed, and while thus engaged over
him, Doyle, it would seem, conceived the fitting
moment to have arrived, proceeded to the fence,
gathered a fence stake, and returning to the two
brothers, struck the sober one over the head, and continued to beat him until he was senseless, literally

knocking out his brains. He then rifled the pockets of the drunken one, and went on a short distance, to a house, where he got something to eat. The pocket book which contained the money was found a few rods distant from the murdered man, in the direction of the house where the murderer stopped. He then went down to Warren station, but not meeting the cars, proceeded to the Junction, where he took the Aurora train for Chicago. He was immediately pursued to the city, information and a description of his person given to the officers, and on Thursday afternoon, deputy sheriff S. E. Bradley arrested him as he was walking in Randolph street. Sheriff Smith was telegraphed of his arrest, and started early on Friday morning and brought him to this place about noon of the same day. The grand jury had not yet adjourned, and an indictment was found against him. In the afternoon he was brought into court, it being still in session, and presented with a copy of the indictment. Having no counsel, the court assigned to him as counsel, R. N. Murray, Esq., assisted by N. Allen, Esq. After consultation with the State's attorney, it was agreed to allow the prisoner to plead to the indictment at the next term of the circuit court, upon which he was committed to jail to await his trial at that time. Coroner Hagemann held an inquest over the body of the murdered man, and the verdict of the jury was that he came to his death by being willfully murdered at the hands of Patrick Doyle. The name of the deceased was Patrick Tole, and he is about 25 years of age. The prisoner is a thin, spare man, about 23 or 24 years of age. There does not appear to have been any feud or quarrel existing between the brothers and Doyle, whatever, nor do they appear to have been in any sort of an affray at the time the crime was committed, which makes the case look still more aggravated."

The following is a list of those who have served the county in the legislature of the state:

1836 — Capt. JOSEPH NAPER,	1848 — WARREN L. WHEATON,
1838 — Capt. JOSEPH NAPER,	1850 — WILLARD T. JONES,
1842 — JEDUTHAN HATCH,	1852 — Capt. JOSEPH NAPER,
1844 — JULIUS M. WARREN,	1854 — E. O. HILLS,
1846 — Capt. E. KINNE,	1856 — TRUMAN W. SMITH.

The following are the names of attorneys who have been connected with the Du PAGE County bar: Nathan Allen, P. Ballingall, C. B. Hosmer, O. B. Bush, James F. Wight, Allen McIntosh, A. R. Dodge, H. Loring, R. N. Murray, H. H. Cody, H. F. Vallette, W. Blanchard, S. F. Daniels, J. C. Waldron, L. E. De Wolf, M. S. Hobson, W. O. Watts.

We close this part of our history by giving the names of the officers of the county from its organization to the present time.

LIST OF COUNTY OFFICERS.

The first election for county officers was held at the Preëmption House, in Naperville, on the first Monday in May, 1839. S. M. Skinner, Stephen J. Scott, and

L. G. Butler were, by law, appointed judges of election. The officers elected at this time served until the general election, Aug. 5th, same year. As the names of supervisors are inserted in the lists of town officers appended to the histories of the several towns, they do not appear in this list.

NAMES OF SHERIFFS.

Elected,

May, 1839—Daniel M. Green.....................Du Page
Aug. 1839—Daniel M. Green.....................   "
Aug. 1842—Harry B. Fowler.....................   "
Aug. 1844—Robert N. Murray.................Naperville
Aug. 1846—George Roush......................   "
Nov. 1850—C. R. Parmalee;.....................Lisle
Nov. 1852—T. W. Smith ....Winfield.
Nov. 1854—A. C. Graves......................   "
Nov. 1856—James J. Hunt.................. ....Naperville

RECORDERS.

May, 1839—S. M. Skinner...................   "
Aug. 1843—A. S. Jones......................   "
Aug. 1847—J. J. Riddler....................   "

In 1849 the clerk of the circuit court was made *ex-officio* recorder, the county court and the office of probate justice were succeeded by the county court, composed of a county judge and two county justices of the peace. The office of county commissioner's clerk was succeeded by county clerk, the county judge and the two county justices sitting together for the transaction of county business, and the county judge, with the clerk, constituting a court for the transaction of probate business. Under this provision, Nathan Allen was elected county judge in 1849, and Charles Gary and Peter Northrup were elected county justices. In 1850 the township organization law was adopted, and the first board of supervisors elected. The following persons have held the office of clerk of the circuit court :

Appointed,
1839—P. Ballingall..........................Naperville
1843—E. B. Bill..............................   "

Elected,
1849—John J. Riddler........................   "
1852—Peter Northrop......................Addison
1856—John Glos.............................Wayne

CLERKS OF COUNTY COMMISSIONER'S COURT, AND COUNTY CLERKS.

Elected,
July 14, 1839—Clark A. Lewis*...............Warrenville
Aug. 5, 1839—Allen McIntosh.................Naperville
Aug.   1843—Allen McIntosh.................   "
Aug.   1847—H. H. Cody....................Bloomingdale

Re-elected,
Aug.   1849—H. H. Cody....................Bloomingdale

Elected,
1853—M. C. Dudley.................Bloomingdale

PROBATE JUSTICES AND COUNTY JUDGES.

Elected,
May, 1839—J. W. Walker.................Downer's Grove
Aug. 1839—Lewis Ellsworth...............Naperville
Aug. 1843—Nathan Allen.................   "
Aug. 1847—J. J. Kimball.................   "
Aug. 1849—Nathan Allen†.................   "
Nov. 1852—Jeduthan Hatch ....Lisle
Nov. 1853.—Walter Blanchard.............Downer's Grove

---

* Died same month, 1839, and vacancy filled by appointment of P. Ballingall.
† Resigned, 1852.

COUNTY TREASURERS.

Elected,

May, 1839 — M. Sleight.............................Naperville
Aug. 1839 — Stephen J. Scott ....   "
Aug. 1843 — R. K. Potter.......................   "
Aug. 1845 — J. J. Kimball....................   "
Aug. 1847 — N. A. Thomas ....   "
Nov. 1849 — H. F. Vallette.....................Milton
Nov. 1851 — H. F. Vallette....................Naperville
Nov. 1853 — H. F. Vallette ....   "
Nov. 1855 — W. J. Johnson...................   "

SCHOOL COMMISSIONERS.

Elected,

1841 — Lewis Ellsworth......................Naperville
1843 — R. N. Murray.........................   "
1844 — Horace Brooks.......................Milton
1847 — W. L. Wheaton.....................   "
1849 — Hope Brown.........................Naperville
1851 —   "   ....   "
1853 —   "   ....   "
1855 —   "   * ....   "

Appointed,

1856 — Lorin Barnes........................Bloomingdale

COUNTY COMMISSIONERS.

Elected,	Elected,
May, 1839 — Josiah Strong,	Aug. 1842 — Warren Smith,
" — H. L. Cobb,	Aug. 1843 — T. Hubbard,
" — T. P. Whipple,	Aug. 1844 — John Thompson,
Aug. 1839 — Hart S. Cobb,	Aug. 1845 — T. Andrus,
" — John W. Walker,	" — John Thompson,
" — Hiram Fowler,	Aug. 1846 — Asa Knapp,
Aug. 1840 — N. Stevens,	Aug. 1847 — S. D. Pierce,
Aug. 1841 — J. A. Smith,	Aug. 1848 — David Crane.

* Resigned, September, 1856.

COUNTY SURVEYORS.

Elected,

May, 1839 — L. Meacham......................Bloomingdale
Aug. 1839 — J. B. Kimball......................Naperville
Aug. 1847 — Horace Brooks......... ....Milton
Nov. 1849 —   "   ....   "
Nov. 1851 —   "   ....   "
Nov. 1853 —   "   ....   "
Nov. 1855 —   "   ....   "

CORONERS.

Elected,

May, 1839 — H. L. Peaslee .:....................Naperville
Aug. 1839 —   "   ....   "
Aug. 1840 — E. G. Wight ....   "
Aug. 1842 — N. Loring........................   "
Aug. 1844 — J. Keefer........................   "
Aug. 1846 — D. C. Gould......................   "
Aug. 1848 — L. Avery........................Milton
Nov. 1849 — C. C. Barnes.....................Naperville
Nov. 1852 — F. C. Hagemann...................Winfield
Nov. 1854 — W. B. Stewart....................Naperville
Nov. 1856 — Alfred Waterman...... ....Wheaton

A HISTORY OF THE TOWN OF MILTON.

THE settlement of this town was commenced in 1831, by Harry T. Wilson and Lyman Butterfield. Mr. Babcock and Thomas Brown settled in the town soon after. They were followed by Joseph Chadwick and his sons.

In 1850 the present township organization law was adopted, and the first town meeting was held at the house of Jesse C. Wheaton, in that year.

The town is situated nearly in the centre of the county, and is six miles square. The Galena and Chicago Union Railroad passes directly through it. The present population is about two thousand. As an agricultural district, this town is unsurpassed, being adapted to all the various branches of farming. It presents a beautiful and varied landscape of prairie and woodland, hill and dale, running brooks and crystal founts. In its present and future prospects, this town affords a picture which some of New England's towns might well envy.

There are two flourishing villages within the limits of this town, Wheaton and Danby. Wheaton is a fine, growing village, beautifully situated on the G. and C. U. Railroad, 25 miles west of Chicago, and 5 miles east of the Junction of the C. B. & Q. Railroad, the Dixon Air Line Railroad, and the St. Charles Branch road ; thus rendering access to the town direct

4*

and easy from all points. Jesse C. and Warren L. Wheaton were the original proprietors of the village, which was laid out by them in 1853. In the fall of 1849 the railroad was completed to this point, and during the following year Messrs. J. G. Vallette, H. H. Fuller, and a Mr. Lynch erected the first buildings. Few improvements were made until it was surveyed and platted in 1853. There are now about 1,000 inhabitants within the village limits, and upward of 200 buildings have been erected. The railroad company erected a commodious building in 1856, for their use as a depot for passengers and freight, in connection with which is an express office. The following list of the business establishments of the town will give some idea of its wants, growth and prosperity, when it is considered that scarcely four years ago there were not more than two or three dwellings to be found in the place. There are now : 1 hotel, 12 stores, 12 factories, including an extensive carriage manufactory, and a steam flouring mill, 2 lightning rod manufactories, 2 lumber yards, 2 markets, 2 post offices, 1 school house, 1 institute, 1 printing office, 1 nursery. The amount of capital employed by the principal business men, varies between three and five thousand dollars, and the annual sales range between ten and fifteen thousand dollars. At the carriage manufactory of Messrs. Chadwick, Brother & Co., some fifteen hands are employed and about fifty carriages of every description made annually. The steam flour mill was built in 1856, by Messrs. Northrop & Watson. This mill has two run of stones, and produces flour of a superior quality.

The Baptist, Wesleyan and Episcopal Methodist denominations each have their respective church organizations, connected with which are Sabbath schools, missionary societies, and various benevolent enterprises. The truly reformatory movements of the day find warm supporters here, so much so that it has been denominated a "reformatory town." The Methodist Episcopal and Wesleyan Methodist churches had their organizations in the town prior to the settlement of the village. The present membership of the Wesleyan church is about 75, and the Rev. Lucius C. Matlack, President of the Illinois Institute, is the pastor. There are about 60 members of the M. E. church, and Rev. B. Close is pastor. The Baptist church of Wheaton was organized on the 12th of November, 1856, by a council from the neighboring churches, with the usual services of church recognition. There are now 17 members of this church. The present pastor is Rev. Mr. Garrison.

A printing office was established here in 1856, from which was issued for several months the DU PAGE COUNTY GAZETTE, by J. A. J. Birdsall. This paper was discontinued in the spring of 1857, for want of sufficient patronage to sustain it.

A military company was organized in this place in 1856, called the "Wheaton Artillery." The officers of the company are John Short, Captain; J. G. Vallette, 1st Lieut.; J. M. Vallette, 2d Lieut. Number of members, 40.

The Illinois Institute is located in this place. It has a liberal charter, conferring powers equal to the best colleges, and embraces academical, collegiate and theological departments of instruction. The charter was granted by the Legislature, in 1855. Forty acres of valuable land and three thousand dollars cash donation, formed the basis of its establishment. The fund has been increased by additional gifts, so that the value of real estate owned by the trustees is now upward of $10,000. The sum of five hundred dollars was raised by subscription, in 1856, with which chemical, philosophical and astronomical apparatus was procured for the institution. Add to these the amount of scholarships sold, which is nearly $20,000, and we have an aggregate of nearly $30,000. This amount is to be offset by a debt of $2,500. So great a success within a little more than three years of its existence, is an encouraging fact, and promises well for the future. It is the design of the trustees to secure to the institution a permanent endowment fund of $100,000, by the sale of scholarships. Its catalogue for the first year numbered 140 students, the second year 270, and its present prospects are more flattering than at any previous period. The following list comprises the faculty of 1856 :

Rev. Lucius C. Matlack, President
G. H. Collier, A.B., Prof. Mathematics and Natural Philosophy.
O. F. Lumry, A.B., Prof. Greek and Latin.
Miss M. A. Newcomb, A.B., Principal Female Department.
Mrs. Minerva Hoes, M.D., Anatomy, Physiology, and Botany.
Sebastian Pfrangle, German and Music.
L. A. Jones, Assistant Teacher.

In connection with the Institute, a commodious boarding hall has been erected, at an expense of nearly $3,000.

There are two post offices in the town, one at Wheaton, and one at the village of Danby. Post master at Wheaton, C. K. W. Howard. At Danby, David Kelly.

There are seven school districts in the town. The original fund derived from the sale of school land was $800. It is now $1,238 82. The public schools are attended by 790 scholars. Township treasurer, L. W. Mills. Few towns in the county have done more than this, to advance the interests of public schools.

Danby is an unusually pleasant and quiet village, beautifully located on the Galena Railroad, about 23 miles west of Chicago. The railroad was completed to this place in the fall of 1849. During the same season the railroad company erected a station house, which was the first frame building put up in the place. In the spring of 1850, the first settlement was made by John O. Vallette. Milo F. Meacham, A. Hantz, W. Wilson, Wm. Waggoner, and Dr. L. Q. Newton, the original proprietor of the town, came in during the following year.

The place has grown rapidly during the last two or three years, and bids fair to rival some of its sister towns of much greater pretensions. Its present population is between three and four hundred. It has 1 hotel, 2 drug stores, 3 dry goods stores, 1 cabinet shop, 1 grist mill, 1 tin and hardware store, 1 blacksmith shop, and 1 lumber yard.

Physicians at Wheaton, O. Wakelee, F. C. Hagemann, J. O. Vallette, Dr. Lowrie, and A. Waterman.

Physicians at Danby, L. Q. Newton, H. S. Potter, and Dr. Saxe.

Attorneys at Wheaton, S. F. Daniels and L. E. DeWolf. Notaries Public, S. F. Daniels and J. G. Vallette, at Wheaton, and Horace Brooks, who is also county surveyor, at Danby.

The following list comprises the names of the town officers of the town of Milton, since its organization:

SUPERVISORS:

1850 — Warren L. Wheaton,	1854 — W. J. Johnson,
1851 — W. J. Johnson,	1855 — "
1852 — "	1856 — F. H. Mather,
1853 — "	1857 — "

TOWN CLERKS.

1850 — Alfred Standish,	1854 — Carlos Johnson,
1851 — J. F. Lester,	1855 — Henry Benjamin,
1852 — J. O. Vallette,	1856 — G. P. Kimball,*
1853 — Carlos Johnson,	1857 — L. W. Mills.

ASSESSORS:

1850 — J. G. Vallette,	1854 — Horace Brooks,
1851 — Horace Brooks,	1855 — "
1852 — "	1856 — D. Balsley,
1853 — "	1857 — J. C. Wheaton.

COLLECTORS:

1850 — Smith Brookins,	1854 — O. Jewell,
1851 — D. L. Christian,	1855 — C. K. W. Howard,
1852 — Andrew Snyder,	1856 — Luther Chadwick,
1853 — Jesse C. Wheaton,	1857 — C. K. W. Howard.

CONSTABLES:

1850 — J. G. Vallette,	1854 — Reubén Hinzen,
1851 — D. L. Christian,	1855 — D. Balsley,
Smith Brookins,	C. K. W. Howard,
1852 — Joseph Mason,	1856 — David Balsley,
1853 — David Brookins,	1857 — "

*Resigned, and vacancy filled by L. W. Mills.

OVERSEERS OF THE POOR:

1850 — Erastus Gary,
1851 — David Capron,
1852 — John Hacket,
1853 — Lester Webster,

1854 — Orlando Wakelee,
1855 — J. G. Vallette,
1856 — J. D. Ackerman,
1857 —   "

JUSTICES OF THE PEACE:

1850 — Erastus Gary, to present time.
   Daniel Fish, "
1853 — Daniel Fish. "

COMMISSIONERS OF HIGHWAYS:

1850 — John Hacket,
  J. C. Wheaton,
  Daniel Fish,
1851 — J. C. Wheaton,
  J. S. Dodge,
  Frank Ott,
1852 — Daniel Fish,
  Erastus Gary,
  Enos Jones,
1853 — A. Snyder,
  Enos Jones,
  J. G. Vallette,

1854 — Thomas Holmes,
  F. H. Mather,
  Jehiel Wright,
1855 — Thomas Holmes,
  N. M. Dodge,
  Jehiel Wright,
1856 — Daniel Fish,
  Greenleaf Ring,
  John Bachelder,
1857 — W. N. Reese,
  H. Hadley,
  Joseph Granger.

A HISTORY OF THE TOWN OF NAPERVILLE.

THE first inhabitant of this town was Capt. Joseph Naper, who came to this state from Ohio, in the winter of 1831. His family arrived in June, of the same year, and occupied a log house, near the present site of the grist mill. The following list includes the names of all we have been able to ascertain, who settled in the town previous to 1838: John Naper, Ira Carpenter, John Stevens, John Murray, M. Hines, A. H. Howard, S. J. Scott, Willard Scott, L. Ellsworth, A. S. Jones, S. Sabin, Geo. Martin. L. C. Aldrich, H. L. Peaslee, R. Hyde, Geo. Stroubler, G. Bishop, J. H. Stevenson, W. Rose, R. Wright, E. G. Wight, J. F. Wight, S. M. Skinner, W. Weaver, J. Granger, N. Crampton, W. J. Strong, R. Whipple, U. Stanley, T. Thatcher, A. T. Thatcher, J. Lamb, R. N. Murray, R. Hill, David Babbitt, H. C. Babbitt, J. S. Kimball, J. B. Kimball, L. Kimball, Harry Fowler, Hiram Fowler, R. K. Potter, J. J. Kimball, Adial S. Jones, Peter Dodd, Nathan Allen, Benjamin Smith.

As the history of the first few years of the settlement of this town has already been given in the general view of the county, a repetition of it is deemed unnecessary in this place. The land in this town is generally level. The soil is productive, and equally favorable to grass and the cultivation of grain. The town abounds in limestone, and furnishes lime in considerable quantities for market in other towns. In the east part of the town, stone of an excellent quality for building purposes is found, and large quantities are quarried for that purpose annually, upon land owned by Joseph Naper and George Martin. Extensive sand beds have also been opened, which yield an abundance of sand of a superior quality.

Although the town is well watered, yet there are no streams of much note, excepting the Du Page river, which runs through it from north to south, on the east side. This stream affords several advantageous mill sites in its course through the town.

Naperville is the oldest town in the county, and the first in point of property and population. It has upward of two thousand inhabitants, 2 hotels, 12 stores, 6 churches, 1 bakery, 1 bank, 2 post offices, 1 grist mill, 10 manufactories, 1 saw mill, 2 breweries, 1 tin and stove warehouse, 1 printing office, 2 quarries, 2 extensive lumber yards, 2 nurseries, and 1 incorporated academy.

The town pays $3,400 annually for the support of preaching, and about $1,500 for the support of common schools. There are 400 members of the different churches, and 350 scholars in the Sabbath schools.

The village of Naperville lies partly in the town of Lisle, being divided by the town line into two unequal parts, the greater lying in the town of Naperville. In our notice of the village, we include the territory lying within its limits in both towns. The first frame building erected here was by A. H. Howard, in the fall of 1833. It was erected a few rods in front of the present dwelling of Mrs. Howard. Among the buildings next put up of this description was the Preëmption

House, by Mr. George Laird, in 1835. This hotel was
owned and under the management of Gen. E. B. Bill,
for several years, during which time no hotel west of
Chicago enjoyed a more extended and well-deserved
patronage. The road passing through the village from
east to west, was the great thoroughfare between
Chicago and Galena, and the town presented the
appearance of an unusually active and business-like
place. At a *very* early date it is said the size of the
town exceeded even that of Chicago! the latter city
having but one log house, while Naperville had *two*.
The first mill constructed upon the river was a saw-
mill, in 1835, which was torn down in 1840, to give
place to the flouring mill which stands upon the same
site. This mill has two run of stones, and enjoys
unsurpassed advantages for water power.

The original town plat was laid out in the year 1835,
by Capt. Naper. The plat embraced about 80 acres.
To the original plat, several additions have since been
made. The usual form of the village lots in the
original plat was four rods front by ten in depth, containing one-fourth acre. These were large, compared
with some which have been laid out in more modern
times. The precise reason for this diminution in size
has never been ascertained with certainty. Several
reasons have been assigned. One presumption is,
that there was formerly more land to the acre than
there now is. Another is, that the land is more valuable than it used to be; but this is controverted by the
fact that the large lots are sold at the same, or lower
prices, than the prices at which the smaller ones are
held. Some think the true reason lies in *persons*, and

not in *property*. No fault, however, can be found with the early proprietors of the town, either in regard to size of lots, or as to the terms on which they were sold. Many lots were given away, and others were sold at low prices, and upon such terms, as to time, that they have not been paid for even to this day. Everything was done in this respect, that could add to the prosperity of the place.

The mercantile business, aside from agriculture, is the chief business of the town. The principal stores employ capitals of between six and eight thousand dollars, and do a business ranging from thirty to fifty thousand dollars, annually. They sell large amounts of goods, not only to the inhabitants of this, but of surrounding towns. Integrity is a marked characteristic of the dealings of the merchants of Naperville. This, in connection with the uniformly low prices at which they sell their goods, has secured to them a liberal and extended patronage.

There are two large nurseries near the village, from which trees and shrubs are sent to all parts of the northwest. We have been furnished some account of the business of these nurseries, which we give below:

The Du Page Eclectic Nurseries were established in 1853, by R. W. and R. M. Hunt. During the four years past these nurseries have propagated, in each year, from fifty to one hundred and fifty thousand fruit trees. Ornamental trees and shrubbery have been proportionally increased, and some thousands of foreign trees and shrubs have been added by importation, as the business has justified. The Du Page County Nurseries, of Lewis Ellsworth & Co., were established in 1849. These nurseries cover at present some fifty acres of ground, embracing in the collection the most extensive stock and assortment of varieties of fruit and ornamental trees, shrubs and plants, to be found in the northwest. The yearly increase of trees and shrubs, by propagation and by importation, is truly astonishing. The proprietors have imported during the present season, from Europe, more than thirty thousand young evergreens and other plants. Attached to the establishment is a plant house, arranged for propagating plants during the winter season. The establishment gives employment to a large number of workmen, some ten families deriving their entire support from it. From fifteen to twenty men are employed, at an expense of over six thousand dollars per annum. During the present year the proprietors have commenced a nursery at Wheaton, where about eight acres of land are occupied, making, in all, sixty acres, cultivated for their business.

There are several other nurseries in the county, but the Du Page County Nurseries are, it is believed, the first in time and the first in importance.

The plow and wagon shop of Messrs. Vaughan & Peck is located in this village. It was originally established by A. S. Jones, who is entitled to the credit of originating the steel plow now so much in use. The manufacture of plows at this shop commenced in 1840. They possess many superior qualities, for which they have become extensively noted throughout the west. From its circular, we learn that "this establishment is one of the oldest in the western states, having manufactured the steel scouring plow for eighteen or twenty years, and never been beaten at any state or county fair." The establishment is capable of making fifteen plows per day. Two thousand five hundred were manufactured in 1856. The average price of these plows is $15 each. Wagons, buggies, and most kinds of agricultural implements are made here. Thirty-six men are employed.

The Bank of Naperville was chartered and went into operation in 1854. Its nominal capital is $500,000. This bank is established upon a basis which renders it as secure as any similar institution in the state, and gives it the full confidence of the public.

There are two breweries in the town, which consume annually fifteen thousand bushels of barley, and eleven thousand pounds of hops, at a cost of ten thousand dollars. From these, one hundred and eighty-six thousand gallons of beer are made, which, at the usual retail price, reaches the enormous sum of one hundred and forty-eight thousand, eight hundred dollars! Although beer is to some extent an article of home consumption, it having in many instances superseded the use of that ancient beverage known by the name of *water*, yet it forms our chief article of export. The sale of this article in some of our neighboring towns is very large.

A few words concerning the process of manufacturing beer may be of interest to some. The barley is first put into large cisterns or vats, which are capable of holding from one hundred to one hundred and fifty bushels. Water is then poured upon it, and in this condition it remains for about two days. It is then spread out about one foot in depth upon the floor of the drying kiln, which consists of an immense oven, so arranged that its temperature can be adjusted to the *germinating point*. Here the process of germinating, or malting, as it is termed, takes place. After this, it is passed through a cleaning machine, and then through a malt machine, by which last process it is ground or broken so that its virtue can be more easily extracted. The malt, as it is then termed, is gathered up and placed in vats holding from fifty to one hundred barrels each, when boiling water is poured upon it. After remaining several hours in this condition, during which time the mixture is constantly agitated by means of long wooden ladles, the liquid portion is drained off and boiled for some time in large boilers prepared for the purpose. This process is repeated three or four times, or until the strength of the barley is all extracted. Hops are then introduced, which give it *body*, and serve to preserve it during the warm season. The liquid is then placed in another large vat, called the cooler, and when its temperature is reduced to the proper point, is drawn off into the work tub, where yeast is introduced, and the finishing process of fermentation begins. By this process all extraneous matter is separated and thrown off, and the liquid comes out *lager beer* "of the first water," impatient to be swallowed.

The Odd Fellows, Masons, and Good Templars have each a society and hall in this place. There was at one time a large society of the Sons and Daughters of Temperance here, but their charter was surrendered in 1854.

The I. O. of O. F. was organized in 1850. The

number of members has been about 60, and the present
number is 48. The present officers of this institution
are S. Boliman, N. G.; W. Naper, V. G.; S. O.
Vaughan, Secretary, and R. Willard, Treasurer.

~ The Masonic Lodge was established in 1848. The
number of all the members to the present time is 120.
There are now about 60 members. The officers are
H. H. Cody, W. M.; C. D. Haight, S. W.; and C.
W. Keith, J. W.

The lodge of the Good Templars was instituted in
June, 1857. There are now 40 members. E. H.
Eyer holds the office of W. C. T.

It might be mentioned in this connection, that the
"Know Nothings" had a lodge somewhere in this
place about a year ago, but their precise locality has
never been fully determined. A list of the members
has been furnished us, but our space will not admit of
its publication. The doings of the society were char-
acteristically covert and sly, so that we are obliged to
admit that we *know nothing* about their movements.

The Naperville Artillery Company was organized
in 1856. There are now some 50 members belonging
to the company. The officers are J. J. Hunt, Capt.;
H. F. Vallette, 1st Lieut.; R. Naper, 2d Lieut.: J.
H. Hobson, 3d Lieut., and E. Page, Ensign.

There are two post offices in the town, one at Naperville, and one at Big Woods. The post master at the
Big Woods is John Warne. The office at Naperville
has an annual income of one thousand dollars; R.
Naper, post master.

There are several valuable public and private libraries in the town. The circulating library of H. C.

Daniels, M. D., contains 400 volumes of miscellaneous reading. There are two school libraries of about 500 volumes, and four Sabbath school libraries, containing about 1,000 volumes. The law library of Messrs. Vallette & Cody contains 500 volumes, and is the largest collection of the kind in the county.

The freshet of 1857 was a calamity to the town. This occurred in March. The river, swollen by the heavy rains and the melting snow, overflowed its banks and inundated all the business portion of the town. Soon after the stream commenced rising, the mill-dam gave way and let down upon the town an avalanche of water, bearing upon its swift current large sheets of ice, which demolished everything in their way. The rise of the water was so sudden that many of the inmates of the houses situated on the banks of the river, with great difficulty escaped. Several buildings, including three stores, were carried away. The loss is variously estimated, between fifteen and twenty thousand dollars, and was chiefly sustained by Messrs. M. Hines, J. T. Green, R. Willard, C. W. Keith and Joseph Naper.

The village of Naperville was incorporated by act of Legislature in the winter of 1857. The first election of officers for the corporation was held in May following. The names of the Board elected at that time are as follows: President, Joseph Naper; Trustees, H. H. Cody, Geo. Martin, M. Hines and X. Eggerman; Police Justice, H. F. Vallette; Constable, A. C. Graves; Assessor, A. W. Colt; Clerk, C. M. Castle.

Our space will not admit of our entering into the details of the ecclesiastical history of this town. The first effort toward organizing a religious society was made by settlers in this and the adjoining town of Lisle, as early as 1833. A meeting was held in Lisle on the 13th of July, in that year, and a society organized by Rev. Jeremiah Porter and Rev. N. C. Clark, missionaries for this county, and Rev. C. W. Babbitt, of Tazewell county. This meeting was called at the request of Isaac Clark, Pomeroy Goodrich, Israel Blodget, Robert Strong, Leister Peet, Henry H. Goodrich, and Samuel Goodrich. The society commenced its labors with true christian zeal, and its numbers rapidly increased. Among the first resolutions adopted by the society, we find the following:

Resolved, That the minister, as soon as practicable, shall visit every family in the settlement, and that each member of the brethren, in turn, when called upon, shall accompany him, to ascertain the state of religious feeling, and to awaken attention to the subject, and especially to explain the object and plan of Sabbath schools, and the distribution of tracts.

Rev. N. C. Clark was the first pastor of the society. Meetings were held during the year at different places in the south part of the settlement, for three Sabbaths in succession, and the fourth in the school house at Naperville. Punctuality in attendance upon the meetings of the society was strictly enjoined, and a committee appointed to notice the absence of any, and call on him at the next meeting, for his *reason*. In 1834, the society raised one hundred dollars to help defray the expenses of their pastor. During the year of 1835 Mr. Clark preached regularly upon the first and fifth Sabbaths of each month at his own house, on the second and fourth at Naperville, and on the third in

5

the neighborhood of Mr. Luther Hatch. He continued
as their pastor until July, 1836. With a pledge of
three hundred dollars, and the assistance of the Home
Missionary Society, the society next secured the services
of Rev. E. Strong, who remained with them until
August, 1837. The Rev. J. G. Porter then became
their pastor, and served the society faithfully and
acceptably until July, 1840, when, at his own solicitation, he was dismissed. During the years of 1838 and
1839 the society began to feel the need of a house of
worship which should be their own. A vote was
passed, at a meeting held in September, 1838, to build
a meeting house, and at a subsequent meeting, in
March, 1839, Naperville was selected as the place for
its location. Deacon Clark, Pomeroy Goodrich, and
Henry Goodrich, were appointed the first trustees.
In October, 1840, Rev. O. Lyman became pastor. He
was employed for six months, or until an opportunity
offered to procure a permanent minister. The Rev.
J. H. Prentiss, of Fulton, received a unanimous call
in November, and was installed as pastor on the 12th
of July, 1842. Three hundred dollars were pledged
for his support, payable half in money and half in produce, by the society, and an additional sum of two
hundred dollars was obtained from the Home Missionary Society. By his own request, his connection with
the society was dissolved, Aug. 25, 1843. Arrangements were then made with Rev. E. W. Champlain,
to preach for the society on each alternate Sabbath
during the remainder of the year, commencing on the
first Sabbath in October. Mr. Champlain continued
as the pastor until his death, February 8th, 1845. At

a meeting of the society, April 18th, 1844, it was resolved "that we deem it expedient to take immediate measures to build a house of worship." At a subsequent meeting, Deacon Isaac Clark, George Blackman, Deacon Pomeroy Goodrich, J. Strong, and Eli Northam, were appointed a committee to select a site. That committee selected a site gratuitously offered by Capt. Morris Sleight. The choice was concurred in by the society, and the present edifice was erected upon it in 1847.

By the death of the Rev. Mr. Champlain the whole society was thrown into mourning. Although he had labored among them for only a brief period, yet he had become endeared to his people by the strongest ties of affectionate regard. He is the only minister of any denomination who has died in this place, or whose sepulcher is with us. After his death the people were destitute of a settled minister for several months, but the pulpit was regularly supplied by Rev. O. Lyman. A call was extended to Rev. Hope Brown, in August, 1845, which was accepted. It was provided that he should preach on alternate Sabbaths, and receive a compensation proportionate to the amount of service rendered. Mr. Brown was connected with the Home Missionary Society, and for several years after his settlement here, received contributions toward his support from that society. He was installed on the 11th of November, 1845, and continued with this people until October, 1856, when he was dismissed, at his own request.

Of Mr. Brown it may be said that few men are better calculated for the Christian ministry. He preached the truth every day by a consistent Christian example, as well as from the pulpit on the Sabbath. In October, 1856, the present pastor, Rev. E. Barber, was invited to the desk. The congregation has considerably increased during the past year, and the society has made new accessions to its numbers. The church was never in a more enterprising and prosperous state than at present. The Sabbath school connected with this church has sixty pupils. The whole number of members, since its organization, is 177; the number now belonging to the church is 62.

From the history of the past may we not learn the importance of faithfully sustaining the institutions and ordinances of the Gospel? All our natural, social, and civil advantages, will avail us little without its influence. As a church, and as a society, is it not our *duty* to lend a strong hand for its support, when

> "The pulpit, in the sober use
> Of its legitimate, peculiar powers,
> Must stand acknowledged, while the world shall last,
> The most important and effectual guard,
> Support, and ornament of virtue's cause."

The worldly wisdom of that man is to be admired, who, though not a professing Christian, refused to purchase a farm in a town in a neighboring state, *because they had no regular preaching there.* "For," said he, "though property is cheap there now, it will always be cheap; it will diminish in value without the restraining and elevating influences of the Gospel."

Much credit is due to those early pioneers for the ready zeal which they have manifested in organizing and sustaining the churches in our midst. Many of them are still among us, but are not to tarry with us long; and when they shall depart, may the cause for which they have labored and sacrificed so much be committed to hands equally zealous and faithful to the sacred trust; for it is a fact, well attested, that nothing will make a people so poor as to try to live without the preaching of the truth.

The Baptist church in Naperville was organized through the instrumentality of the Rev. Morgan Edwards, in 1843. At the time of its organization, there were nine members. Immediate steps were taken to erect a house of worship. A building was commenced on the foundation of the present Congregational church, but a difficulty arose between the owner of the lots (who had not yet conveyed them to the society) and one of its members. In consequence of this the owner refused to give title to the society, and forbade the removal of the partly constructed building, threatening personal violence to any one who should attempt it. A committee waited upon him and endeavored to obtain his promised deed of the lots, but it was refused. Finding all their overtures in vain, a large number of the most prominent citizens of the place met by agreement, and unawed either by threats of violence or the terrors of the law, forcibly took down and removed the edifice to its present site, which was donated to the society by Lewis Ellsworth, Esq. In 1844, the building was so far advanced that it was occupied by the Congregational and Baptist societies, each on alternate Sabbaths. Rev. Riley B. Ashley became pastor of this church in

January, 1844, and continued to supply the pulpit
until January, 1846, during which time the church
increased to thirty-six in numbers. From July, 1846,
to July, 1848, Rev. Allen Gross was pastor, and the
church increased to fifty-six. He was succeeded by
the Rev. Silas Tucker, in October, 1848. Mr. Tucker
continued as pastor until October, 1855, when the
number of members was ninety-five. The Rev. Silas
Kenny supplied the desk for eight months during 1856
and 1857. The present pastor is Rev. E. P. Barker.
In 1847 the church was enlarged and improved. Its
present dimensions are 52 feet in length by 36 in width.
At the time it was enlarged, a belfry and steeple were
built upon it, from which sounded the first church bell
in the county. During the past year much has been
done by this society to beautify the church building
and grounds. The Sabbath school connected with this
church numbers about fifty scholars. The doctrines
of modern spiritualism have been embraced by some
of the leading members of this society. Whether
this has contributed to the growth or decay of true
piety in the church, we are not to determine.

The German Evangelical Association has a large
society in this place. This society was formed in 1837,
by a few members from Warren county, Pa. J. C.
Gros, M. Weis, Adam Knopff, George Stroubler, John
Rahm, Martin Asher and Adam Schwigert were
among the first members. Meetings were held in
different parts of the town for several years, until the
church was erected at Naperville, in 1842. The lot
on which the present church stands, was given to the
society by Capt. Naper. Since 1840, the society has

sustained regular preaching, and the church has increased rapidly in numbers. There are now upward of two hundred belonging to the society. Connected with this church there is a Sabbath school of nearly 200 scholars. It has a library of 300 volumes. The present church building is much too small for the accommodation of the society, and the erection of a fine brick edifice is contemplated during the present year. No other church in the county has met with so great a degree of prosperity. We give the names of the pastors, from its organization:

1837 — Rev. Jacob Boas,
1838 — " Martin Hawert,
1839 — " Christian Einsel,
1840 — " J. Lutz,
1841 — " Adam Strooh, C. Lintner,
1842 — " F. Wahl, G. A. Blank,
1843 — " C. Kopp,
1844 — " C. Lintner,
1845 — " G. A. Blank,
1846 — " C. Kopp, S. Dickower,
1847 — " C. Augenstin, G. Meszmer,
1848 — " C. Holl, H. Weilty, J. Raggerts,
1849 — " S. A. Tobias, C. A. Schnackn,
1850 — " B. Apley, M. Hawert,
1851 — " J. Riegal, G. Franzen,
1852 — " " J. Trombaner,
1853 — " G. A. Blank,
1854 — " J. P. Kramer,
1855 — " " J. Gibeis,
1856 — " W. Straczburger,
1857 — " " H. Henitzn.

The Methodist society was formed in 1841, through the instrumentality of J. Granger, A. Keith, Mr. Underwood, E. Rich, and H. Daniels. A church was

built in 1849. The society has been regularly supplied
with pastors since 1841. The Sabbath school connected with this church has about 100 scholars, and
its library contains 250 volumes. There are now
between thirty and forty members belonging to the
society.

NAMES OF PASTORS:

1841 — Rev. Caleb Lamb,	1850 — Rev. M. P. Hannah,
1842 — " John Nason,	1851 — " John Beggs,
1844 — " O. Walker,	1852 — " J. C. Stoughton,
1846 — " Elisha Springer,	1853 — " Mr. Vance,
1848 — " Nathan Jewett,	1854 — " O. Huse,

1856 — Rev. B. Close.

The Catholics have a large society here. Their
church was organized in 1846, and a house of worship
erected during the same year. The society was formed
under the labors of the Rev. Mr. Theroler, and the
first members were Peter Shultz, Xavier Eggerman,
D. Bapst, S. Dutter and G. Ott. In 1852 the church
building was enlarged, for the accommodation of the
rapidly increasing society, which now numbers 232.
The names of the priests who have officiated since
1848, are Rev. Mr. Yung, Rev. Mr. Foelker, who died
here in 1850, Rev. Mr. Zucher, Rev. John Kramer,
Rev. Mr. Etafer, who died here in 1855, and Rev. Mr.
Keiser, who, having been suspended for misdemeanor,
left the community very abruptly sometime in August, 1857.

The physicians at Naperville are H. C. Daniels, J.
Jassoy, W. B. Stewart, R. K. Potter, Dr. Overholser
and Dr. Ferris.

The practicing attorneys are H. F. Vallette and H.

H. Cody, of the firm of Vallette & Cody; W. Blanchard and M. Hobson, of the firm of Blanchard & Hobson. J. F. Wight, for many years the only attorney in the place, has now retired from practice.

Early attention was given by the settlers to the subject of education. A school house was the result of the first public enterprise. In the fall of 1831, a log house was erected on land now owned by Mr. Samuel Boliman, and a school taught there during the following winter by Mr. Leister Peet. The building was by no means remarkable for architectural beauty, but being fourteen feet square, it afforded accommodations to the children of this sparsely settled district for two or three years. Boards were fastened to the sides of the room for desks, and slab benches were provided for seats. Mr. Peet was succeeded by Mrs. Hines and Mr. Hiram Standish, who in succession swayed the scepter of that first temple of incipient liberty, and taught the young idea how to shoot. Some of our most prominent citizens remember well the *rude-a*-mental lessons which they received in the old log shool house, and the introduction of Parley's Magazine, from which they were instructed in almost every department of science, although the time-honored edifice has long since gone to decay. A new frame building for school purposes was erected near where the Congregational church now stands, in 1835. It was used as a church, town house, and two or three terms of the circuit court were held in it before the court house was built. This school house was sold by the district, and for several years previous to the passage of our present school law, the district was

destitute of a school building, and the public schools
of Naperville were of little benefit to the community.
They were usually held for only a small portion of the
year, at places the most inconvenient and uncomfortable. But a new impulse has been given to public
sentiment on the subject of education. There is now
a fine stone building on the west side, belonging to
that district, and a commodious brick building in
process of erection on the east side, for the accommodation of the Lisle district.

The Naperville Academy was incorporated in 1851.
Mr. N. F. Atkins was the first preceptor, and performed
the duties of principal for about one year. After his
removal, the trustees appointed Mr. C. W. Richmond,
then principal of the academy at Great Barrington,
Mass., to fill the vacancy. In this academy, in
addition to the common branches of an English education, instruction is afforded in the languages and
natural sciences, including music, drawing and painting. This institution has sent out many competent
teachers for our public schools. Upward of 600
different scholars have been members of the school
during the past three years. The average attendance
has been about 100. The following are the names of
assistants in the school: Howard Kennedy, A. M.;
Geo. Hudson, J. H, Edson, Mrs. C. W. Richmond,
Mrs. H. L. Snyder, Miss M. B. Dewey, Miss C. E.
Crossman, Prof. C. N. V. Vasque and Eugene Burnell.
The academy building is pleasantly situated in the
west part of the village, is three stories high, and
constructed of durable and handsome stone, found in
the vicinity, at a cost of about six thousand dollars.

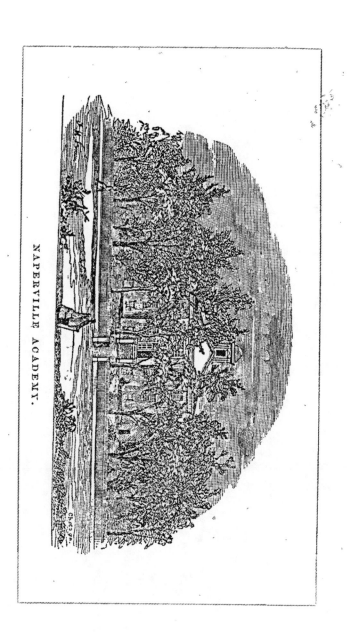

NAPERVILLE ACADEMY.

The institution is provided with chemical, philosophical, geographical and historical charts, and has a library connected with it of about 600 volumes. Few seminaries offer better facilities to students who are pursuing either the English course or preparing for the higher course of collegiate studies.

There are twelve school districts in the town, all of which are provided with good school houses, in which schools are taught from six to ten months during the year. The summer term is usually taught by females, and the winter by males.

There is a private school taught in the family of Mr. Lewis Ellsworth, by Miss S. B. Skinner. The number of pupils is limited to about twelve. Young ladies are here instructed in the English and modern languages, and also in music, drawing and painting.

Our educational facilities, as a town, can not well be surpassed. They are sufficiently ample, and none need grow up in ignorance for want of proper advantages to obtain an education; yet there are many, even at this day, who refuse to avail themselves of the opportunities offered. This is especially the case in the village, but it is hoped that the new buildings which have been recently erected will draw into the schools a large class of the foreign population, who would otherwise go uneducated. Next in importance to the church, our schools should be nourished with peculiar care. The school fund of the town is now $1035 27. For building and repairing school houses, the amount raised by tax and expended in 1853, was $120; in 1854, $209; in 1855, $294; in 1856, $2376; in 1857, $1326. The whole number of pupils in 1856 was 861.

The school section was sold in 1842, at $1 25 per acre.
The present trustees are H. Bristol, F. Myer and H.
Vaughn.   Treasurer, Chas. Hunt.

In what now constitutes the west part of this town,
and prior to the organization, when known as Big
Woods precinct, the offices of justice of the peace
and constable were held by the following named persons: justices of the peace, W. J. Strong, Abel Keys,
John Stolp, David Meeker, Charles Hunt, S. S. Paxton; constables, Allan Williams, C. M. Vaughn, J.
H. Paxton, A. F. Stolp, O. C. Stolp.

List of town officers of the town of Naperville for
the different years since the adoption of the township
organization law:

SUPERVISOR:

1850 — Russel Whipple.	1854 — David Hess.
1851 — "	1855 — R. N. Murray.
1852 — Joseph Naper.	1856 — Charles Hunt.
1853 — Hiram Bristol.	1857 — N. Crampton.

TOWN CLERK:

1850 — C. F. Tarbox.	1854 — Charles Hunt.
1851 — Charles Hunt.	1855 — "
1852 — "	1856 — "
1853 — "	1857 — "

ASSESSOR:

1850 — Enos Coleman.	1854 — A. T. Thatcher.
1851 — "	1855 — A. W. Colt.
1852 — Hiram Bristol.	1856 — David Brown.
1853 — Enos Coleman.	1857 — George Bristol.

COLLECTOR:

1850 — Willard Scott.
1851 — John Stolp.
1852 — Thaddeus Scott.
1853 — Sidney Powers.

1854 — Sidney Powers.
1855 — A. T. Thatcher.
1856 — R. N. Davis.
1857*

OVERSEER OF THE POOR:

1850 — John Warne.
1851 — H. C. Daniels.
1852 — S. L. Jackson.
1853 —   "

1854 — Hiram Branch.
1855 — M. Hines.
1856 — H. C. Daniels.
1857 —   "

COMMISSIONERS OF HIGHWAYS:

1850 — Samuel Rickert,
        H. C. Daniels,
        Enos Coleman.
1851 — Langdon Miller,
        W. J. Strong,
        Samuel Rickert.
1852 — W. J. Strong,
        David Brown,
        A. S. Sabin.
1853 — W. J. Strong,
        A. T. Thatcher,
        David Brown.

1854 — S. L. Jackson,
        Jacob Saylor,
        U. D. Stanley.
1855 — S. M. Babbitt,
        H. Bristol,
        D. B. Rogers.
1856 — C. H. P. Lyman,
        Hiram Bristol,
        Jacob Saylor.
1857 — Hiram Bristol,
        Solomon Givler,
        John Stolp.

JUSTICES OF THE PEACE:

1850 — Charles Hunt,
        Willard T. Jones.
1851 — H. Loring.†
1852 — Charles Hunt,
        H. Loring.

1853 — Harrison Loring.
1854 —   "
        J. J. Riddler.
1855 — Charles Hunt.‡
1856 — Eli Rich.

---

* Collector not elected, it being a tie vote.
† Elected in place of Willard T. Jones, resigned.   ‡ Vice Loring, resigned.

CONSTABLES :

1850 — Sidney Powers,   1852 — S. M. Cole.
         D. C. Butler.   1853 —   "
1851 — Sidney Powers,   1854 — George Stroubler, jr.
         S. M. Cole.   1855 — David Salisbury.
                  1856 — Fred. S. Crane.

A HISTORY OF THE TOWN OF LISLE.

THIS is the oldest town in the county, having been first settled by Bailey Hobson, in the fall of 1830. Among the early settlers were J. C. Hatch, Isaac Clark, Pomeroy Goodrich, John Thompson, John Sargent, Lewis Ellsworth, Thomas Jellies, Martin Asher, J., C., H:, and L. Stanley, E. Bush, Mr. Willard, Henry Puffer, A. B. Chatfield, John Naper, and R. M. Sweet. The increase of population has been in about the same ratio as that of the other towns in the county. It contains now about 1500 inhabitants, of which there is a fair sprinkling of Germans. The town may be regarded as a very intelligent and moral, and relatively considered, religious population. Many of the first settlers came from New England, and brought with them the principles, practices, morals and opinions for which the people of that section have so long been widely and favorably known.

This remark perhaps applies more truthfully to the inhabitants of that division of the town called "The East Branch" than to any other portion of it. The first settlers here, with scarcely an exception, were of the class referred to. They came possessed of a spirit of genuine Christian philanthropy, which prompted them to labor zealously for the good of their fellow men. They were impelled by no narrow, bigoted views of Christian brotherhood and duty, but recognized that great moral principle which first found utterance on

Plymouth Rock, of "freedom to worship God."
Among the pioneers of this class who are now living,
Deacon Isaac Clark, and Deacon Pomeroy Goodrich,
may be mentioned as having labored here for more
than twenty years, with unfailing Christian ardor, for
the upbuilding of the church of Christ. They were
chiefly instrumental in effecting the first religious
organization in the county, which was as early as
1833. The society then formed rapidly increased, by
members from this and the adjoining towns, and as
the country became more thickly settled it was
divided, and separate organizations formed. A notice
of the original society will be found in the history of
the town of Naperville.

In consequence of its being peopled by the class
referred to, correct moral principles have been infused
into the East Branch community, and it would be difficult to find a better state of society, or a more cultivated, intelligent, moral, and industrious class of
citizens, than reside in this section of the town of
Lisle.

The inhabitants are chiefly devoted to agriculture.
The farmers generally have large and highly cultivated
farms, and are in independent circumstances. Land
is held at from twenty-five to fifty dollars per acre,
the price varying according to locality and nature of
soil. Among the best farms upon the east branch are
those of James C. Hatch, John Thompson, D. H.
Naramore, Pomeroy Goodrich, Daniel M. Green,
William B. Green, A. S. Barnard, A. Morse, and
Charles H. Goodrich.

The pioneers of this town had many privations to

undergo, but these were endured and at last conquered by manly courage and enterprise.

A spirit of cordial sociability, friendly sympathy and intercourse prevailed among the early settlers, which, it is feared has lost something of its charms since the country has become more densely populated.

We have frequently heard it remarked by our pioneer mothers, that the pleasantest period of their lives was when they lived in the old log house, of one apartment, which served as kitchen, parlor, pantry, bedroom, wood house and cellar. Sociability was then untrammeled by forms and ceremonies, and the question of "What shall we eat and wherewithal shall we be clothed," was thought to have a more spiritual application than in modern times.

Mrs. Scott made a "party" at an early day, to which all her neighboring friends were invited. For supper she placed before her guests a prodigious loaf of corn bread, the material for which had been prepared by grinding the corn between two stones. Although the repast was pronounced by all most delicious, yet it was entirely eclipsed by that of Mrs. Hobson, who had her "party" soon after, and entertained her guests, not with corn bread *alone*, but *corn bread and molasses* graced her festive board.

The following details will serve to show something of the trials endured by our early settlers, and the heroic fortitude with which they braved discouragements.:

About the middle of May, 1830, Baley Hobson, weary of the toil of clearing the encumbering forests from the rugged banks of the Ohio river, and animated

by the hope of finding a home in the wilderness of the
northwest, more congenial to the spirit and genius of
agriculture, set out from the sparsely settled county of
Orange for the more sparsely settled section of northern Illinois. His resolutions were those of the pioneers
of the west. Without arms amounting to more than
a jack-knife, for defense, he mounted his horse, and
destitute of chart or compass, groped his way, as best
he could, through the dense forests and deep ravines,
and forded the bridgeless waters that lay in his course.
Day after day was consumed in the solitary windings
from hut to hut, through a region which then presented
but slight indications of that civilization which has
since struck its roots deep into the bosom of those
forests. Rain and sunshine alternately poured through
the darkening foliage that overarched his pathway.
Many miles were traveled where not a sound broke
the silence of the dim woods, save the tread of his own
steed as it bore him onward. The dismal surroundings
of a forest path accompanied him until state lines were
crossed, and the bright opening prairies were gained
in the state of Illinois. Emerging from the heavy
timber country of Indiana, into the prairie wilderness,
was an agreeable respite from the dull monotony of
the scenery through which he had passed.

Here was a spot fit for a moment's pause, to view
with far-strained vision those undulating plains, in
contemplating which

> The heart swells, while the dilated sight
> Takes in the encircling vastness.

Moving onward to the north with the hope of success brightening before him, he gained the south bank

of the Illinois river, which he crossed in a ferry-boat at a place then called Ft. Clarke, near the present site of Peru. At this place he fell in company with four strangers, who had been spending some time in exploring the country further west, which they found, comparatively speaking, a blank wilderness, peopled only by savages. Discouraged at the idea of settling in a country so wild and so remote from civilized man, they had abandoned their journey and were returning, with not the most favorable impressions of the great west. They urged Mr. Hobson to abandon the idea also, not only as impracticable, but as a wild and hazardous undertaking. He however left them, and pushed onward, soon reaching Weed's Grove, since known as Holderman's grove, where he found a settlement consisting of five little huts, occupied by as many families. Here, for the first time in his journey, he made a halt, and explored the Du Page river as far as Walker's grove, near Plainfield. He afterwards explored Fox river as far as Long grove, and finally made a claim six miles from Holderman's, and three miles from the main village of the Pottawattomie Indians, on Fox river. In order to secure his claim while moving his family out to it, he cut logs for the erection of what in later times has been termed the "squatter's hut." Having done this, he mounted his horse and turned homeward. To save distance, he took a new route, and struck out upon the unknown prairies, where the footprints of neither man nor beast were to be seen, without a solitary thing to guide him, save the instinctive allurements of his own fireside, which was more than four hundred miles distant.

About noon of the same day he re-crossed the Illinois river, at the lower rapids, and pursued his way until night shut in upon him, when he pitched his camp, consisting of a horse blanket and overcoat, on the banks of a small stream that flowed along the border of a grove. During the night there was a heavy fall of rain, which put out his fire, and for the remainder of the night he was obliged to hold himself in a defensive attitude against the ravenous mosquitoes. The sun rose bright and clear next morning, and he pressed onward. Late in the afternoon he overtook a company of Kickapoo Indians, who were returning from a hunting excursion, and accompanied them to their village, where he was fortunate enough to find a white man, a trader, with whom he passed the night. Leaving the wigwam town early next morning, he laid his course over the trackless prairie, for the waters of the Sangamon, which were reached just as the sun went down. Here, for the first time in three day's travel, he struck the trail of his former course. A cabin stood on the bank of the stream, occupied by a family whose nearest neighbors were twelve miles distant. He passed the night with them, and after breakfast the next morning, re-crossed the river which he had left some five weeks previous. Retracing his former path over the wide prairies of Illinois and through the dense forests of Indiana, he reached his home about the first of July. On the first day of September, in the same year, he started with his family, accompanied by L. Stewart, for his new claim amid the wilds of the northwest. They had proceeded scarcely half a mile when the wagon was upset, and the entire "bag and baggage" strewn promiscuously upon the ground. This was by no means a welcome omen of the invisible future, and created unpleasant forebodings of what might lie before them in their perilous journey. Four hours detention was the result of this first ill fortune. After the wagon was turned right side up, and their effects gathered together, they moved on again. They soon lost sight of things which had grown familiar by time, and the forest through which they passed opened upon them new scenes. The camp fire was kindled whenever night overtook them, and a small canvas tent was their only protection from the inclemency of the weather, and all that screened the starlight and moonbeams from their pillows.

The evening of the third day found them at the Drift Wood fork of the White river. This was now to be crossed. It was a difficult stream, without bridge or ferry, and having a bed of quicksand. As there was but one plan to choose, ("Hobson's choice," of course), they resolved to hazard the experiment of fording. So, increasing the load of the already burdened team with their own weight, and giving the oxen a few smart blows with the braid of buckskin, they dashed into the stream, and with great effort reached the opposite bank. The men were obliged to re-cross the stream for the herd of cattle and horses that were left behind, and the journey was resumed, until the shadows of night compelled them to pitch their tents. Thus they journeyed, day after day, leaving no visible evidence of their passage, save here and there the ashes of their camp fires, fording all the

streams that lay in their course, until they came to
the Wabash, which they crossed in a ferry, two miles
above Terre Haute.

Coming upon the prairies, the land was marshy for
a considerable distance, and their progress was slow
and difficult; but nothing of moment occurred until
they arrived at the Black Swamp, which was about
half a mile in width. Here they were obliged to take
everything from the wagon and carry to the opposite
side on foot. Mrs. Hobson rode across on horseback,
with her babe, and the two little boys waded through
the mire, at the imminent hazard of being entirely
swallowed up. This passed, they journeyed on, encountering similar obstacles, often getting mired, and
often being obliged to unload a part of their goods in
order to proceed. Leaving the Ft. Clarke road, and
having no path to guide them, they now passed through
an uninhabited region for the distance of one hundred
miles, finding but one habitation during six days, and
being able to obtain neither wood nor water to cook
their meals more than twice during the whole time.
Arriving at the Illinois river, they crossed that stream
at the lower rapids, and after traveling a few miles
further, fell in company with Mr. Clark, whose father
resided at Walker's grove. Preparations were being
made for a night encampment, but Clark insisted that
they should go as far as Holderman's grove, where
he intended to remain that night. Having with him
three yoke of oxen, he attached two of them to Mr.
Hobson's wagon, and thus assisted, they went on,
arriving at Holderman's grove at about midnight,
having been on the road twenty-one days. Here they

remained three weeks, during which time Mr. Hobson sowed some fall wheat, cut some hay for his cattle, and began the erection of a cabin on his new claim.

The family were moved to the claim, and lived in a tent until the cabin was so far completed as to admit of their occupying it. Their provisions were likely to run short, and Mr. Hobson set out on horseback to procure some. After spending two days in fruitless search of something to prevent starvation, he returned home. In a few days, he started again on a longer journey, crossing the Fox and Vermilion rivers, the latter of which he forded, where the water covered the back of his horse. Still onward he went, and after crossing the Illinois, and arriving at the Ox Bow prairie, he found he could purchase no flour, but pork was offered him, which he engaged, appointed the time when he would come for it, and returned.

Not feeling entirely satisfied with his location, he resolved to examine the country still further, and accordingly set out in the direction of Fox river. Knowing that a solitary Frenchman was living in a grove near that stream, he thought to reach his hut, if possible, before night-fall; but the darkness came on before he was able to find it, and tying his horse to a tree, he laid down upon the ground, and, with nothing to shield him from the cold of a November night, save his overcoat and horse blanket, slept till morning. On waking, he found, to his surprise, that he had encamped in full sight of the Frenchman's dwelling, but was separated from it by a swamp. It being very cold, he hastened to the cabin, but found the door closed and fastened. He however effected

6

an entrance by descending the chimney, encountering
in his descent some smoke, considerable soot, a blazing
fire, and last, but not by any means least, a huge bull-
dog, who bristled up savagely at the singular phenom-
enon. He made peace with the dog, and sat down to
warm himself by the fire. The proprietor of the cabin
soon returned, and was not a little surprised, on opening the door, at finding a strange guest within.
After breakfasting, Mr. Hobson made his way across
the country to the Du Page river, examining the lands
and localities as far as the site of his present family
residence. This place satisfied him in every respect,
and he at once determined to abandon the claim he
had already made, and secure this as his future home.
He made a few marks by which to identify it, and
returned to his family, having been absent five days.

In a few days, Hobson and Stewart both set out for
the new claim, for the purpose of cutting timber and
building a cabin upon it. This was in December.
They arrived at the Du Page, and found it frozen
over. Unable to force their team into the crusted
stream, they waded through it themselves, breaking
a path in the ice, which the oxen were made to
follow. Having succeeded in crossing, they pitched
their tent, built a fire, and made preparations for
passing the night. During the night it commenced
snowing, and continued throughout the next day.
They attempted to work, but were unable to accomplish anything in consequence of the severity of the
weather, which continued to increase until they were
obliged to abandon their undertaking. They drove
down the river, a distance of three miles, to the dwell-

ing of Mr. Scott, who had built a cabin and moved into it a few days before. Here they passed the night, and the following day and night. On the third day the wind ceased, the severity of the weather somewhat abated, though still very cold, and they started toward home. Their course lay across a prairie for thirty miles, on which there was no appearance of a road, but they accomplished the distance, reaching home before midnight, nearly exhausted by fatigue, hunger and cold. In the course of a few days the weather changed; some rain fell which melted the snow, and by a succession of snow, rain and frost which followed, the earth was covered with a crust of ice, which made traveling almost impossible.

It was now near Christmas, the time at which Mr. Hobson had agreed to go for his pork.

He therefore left his family and stock in care of Mr. Stewart, and set out for Ox Bow prairie with the intention of returning in about ten days. The weather was now extremely cold, and on the afternoon of the second day it commenced snowing. The storm came so fast and thick that the track was soon covered, and he had nothing to direct his course, while the atmosphere was so filled with the falling flakes that he could see only a few feet before him. Toward night a horseman passed him, but said nothing, and was very soon out of sight, leaving no traces of his course, as the snow filled the horse's track almost as soon as made. Night closed in upon him, with no cessation of the driving storm. Unable to see his way even a rod before him, the chance of reaching a habitation, or place of shelter seemed hopeless, and he was about to resign himself to his fate, when he discovered a light at a little distance which appeared to be coming toward him. On its nearer approach, to his inexpressible joy and gratitude, he discovered two or three men, who had come to his assistance, from the nearest settlement. They had been made acquainted with his situation by the horseman who passed him in the afternoon. They assisted him in reaching the settlement, where he stayed till next morning, when, the storm having considerably abated, he started on his way.

He followed a small stream, though it was not his direct course, in order to be nearer the timber and nearer habitations. Before night came on, guided by the barking of dogs, he was enabled to reach a dwelling. Finding it unoccupied, he took temporary possession. A few embers were still burning on the hearth, and taking some rails from the fence he reduced them to fuel and built a fire. He found feed for his oxen, and a supply of provisions for himself, of which he partook without much ceremony, and in peaceful and quiet possession passed the night.

Pursuing his journey next morning, he shortly arrived at another dwelling, where he found the owner of the cabin in which he had stayed the night before, and told him of the liberty he had taken. Being assured that all he had done at the cabin was right, he pressed on and reached his destination on the evening of the fourth day. The pork was procured, and he started homeward on the following morning, his team consisting of two yoke of heavy cattle, and his load, of about one thousand pounds, including a prairie plow.

The snow had fallen to such a depth that he found it impossible to proceed, and was obliged to employ a man with an additional team to assist him on. With the three yoke of oxen attached to the wagon they started, going before with wooden paddles to shovel the snow from the path. About two hours before sunset, they found that in the course of the whole day, they had advanced just one mile! There was little use in trying to go on, so they turned their team and took the back track for a quarter of a mile to a dwelling. Here they remained for a few days, endeavoring to fit the wagon to runners, but in this they were unsuccessful. Mr. Hobson now resolved on trying to reach home on foot, and accordingly set out. He had to cross a twelve mile prairie before coming to a settlement. This he aimed to do in one day, but the sun had passed the meridian before he had made a third of the distance. Knowing it was vain to attempt to gain the settlement, he retraced his steps to the dwelling he had left in the morning, where he arrived, with life and strength nearly exhausted. Here he remained a few days, hardly knowing what course to pursue. Having already been absent many days longer than he had intended, he felt great anxiety for his family, whom he had left but scantily provided with provisions, and at length determined upon making another effort to reach home. Leaving his team and load, with orders, that if it became necessary, the meat should be cut up and salted, he set out in a new direction, pursuing his way through the groves

towards the Illinois river, and finding shelter at night
in the cabins which at long intervals were scattered
through the forests. At length, he arrived at the
Illinois, which he found frozen and covered with snow.
To facilitate progress he now traveled upon the ice
for thirty miles, in imminent peril of his life. The
ice, in many places, was so thin that it gave way beneath his feet. At the end of this distance the river
was open in consequence of its junction with a large
spring, and he was now obliged to travel again
through the deep and drifted snow. His progress
was slow and fatiguing, but impelled by anxiety for
the loved ones at home, he journeyed on with unflag-
ing zeal, and at last reached home on the nineteenth
day of his absence, to the almost overwhelming joy
and surprise of his destitute family, from whom the
last, lingering hope of ever beholding him again had
faded out. Imagine his feelings as his little ones, half
famished, came around him anxiously inquiring about
his wagon, and about the provisions which they expected he would bring to them. Until now he had
borne up against a tide of adverse circumstances with
a determined and even a cheerful spirit, but the situation of his family, with no prospect of relief, was a
matter not to be contemplated without the most dis-
tressing apprehensions. Nearly a week passed, and
the weather became so much moderated that the
snow began to melt, and it was feared that a thaw
was about to commence, in which case their situation
would be rendered still more hopeless. Corn was
their only article of food, and upon this alone they
had already subsisted for more than two months;

this they prepared by hulling and boiling. Something must be done, for starvation seemed looking them in the face. But one plan suggested itself to Mr. Hobson, and that was a hard one to execute. It was to leave his family, and accompanied by Stewart, make one more effort to get his provisions home before the breaking up of the ice. His situation was indeed a trying one. It was with great reluctance that he resolved to leave his family alone and unprotected in the dead of winter, and in a region inhabited only by Indians, whose proximity produced no more agreeable impression than fear, to say the least. But Mrs. Hobson, brushing the tears from her face, and summoning all the courage and resolution she could command, entreated him to go, and leave her to do the best she could. After preparing fuel sufficient to last until their return they set out, taking with them a yoke of cattle which they drove in advance, for the purpose of breaking a road through the snow. Thirteen head of cattle and three horses were left in Mrs. Hobson's care. On the second day after the departure of Messrs. Hobson and Stewart, it commenced snowing and continued without interruption for two days and nights, covering the earth upon a level, three feet deep. On the third day, just at sunrise, the wind began to blow with fury from the west, and continued like a hurricane, without cessation, for three days, sweeping the snow from the ground and piling it in drifts twenty, thirty, and even forty feet high, while the atmosphere was so thick with the driving snow, as almost to turn daylight into darkness. On the first morning of the wind storm, Mrs. Hobson, taking a

pail, went to a spring a few yards from the house for
some water, but before reaching the house she was
compelled to throw the water upon the ground and
make all possible haste back. The children opened
the door for her, which, being in the west side of the
house, it required all their strength to close again. It
was not opened again until after the storm had subsided. The snow, which was constantly driving into
the house, supplied them with water; but who shall
describe the feelings of that mother, as alone with her
little ones, the days dragged wearily along, while her
mind was filled with the most fearful aprehensions.
Husband or brother she should in all probability see
no more. Her children might perish in her sight,
while a like fate awaited herself. It was, indeed, a
severe trial of endurance, and needed all the fortitude
of her soul to sustain such agonizing reflections while
the raging storm swept around her solitary dwelling.
After the wind had ceased, Mrs. Hobson went out to
look after the cattle and horses, but could discover
nothing of them, and concluded they had been covered
in the snow-drifts and perished. The day passed
without any of them making their appearance. The
next morning they all came around from the east side
of the grove, whither they had fled and remained
during the storm. The fuel which had been prepared
and put in the house was now exhausted, while that
which had been left outside was embedded in a deep
snow drift. The only alternative was to dig this wood
out of the snow with a pick-ax, and Mrs. Hobson
accordingly set about it, working and resting alternately, as her strength would permit. Weak and

faint from hunger, and with hands frozen and blistered, she worked on day after day, unable to get out more wood than would barely serve from one day to another. A cow, that was accustomed to being fed at the door came into the house one day and seemed to reel, as if about to fall. Mrs. Hobson pushed her outside of the door, when she immediately fell dead. Fearing that the wolves, which were very plenty and hungry, would come to the door to feed upon the carcass, she covered it deep in the snow.

On the fourteenth day after his departure, Hobson returned with some provisions, leaving Stewart at Holderman's grove with a part of the oxen that were unable to finish the trip. On his arrival, he found the wood which they had prepared, all consumed, and Mrs. Hobson tearing down a log stable and chopping it up for fuel. During that fourteen weary days, Mrs. Hobson had not seen a human being besides her children. Though it was known at Holderman's grove that they were alone, yet no one dared venture to see what had become of them. It was thought by all there that the family would inevitably perish. In the course of eight days Stewart arrived with the remainder of the oxen. They presented a deplorable spectacle indeed, being worn with fatigue, their flesh sore and bleeding, and the hair all cut from their legs by wading through the hard crusted snow. The drifting of the snow had been altogether favorable to the return of Hobson and Stewart. Having arrived at their destination before the wind storm, they remained until they could make themselves some sledges. On the way home, they could travel sometimes the whole day with-

*6

out the crust giving way, and some days their teams would break through every little while, when they were obliged to dig them out again.

At home again, it was now time for new arrangements to be made, as there had been nothing done as yet, upon the new claim. Stewart, accordingly, set out for the new location with the intention of working there, but soon after his arrival the snow went off with a heavy rain.. After the flood, occasioned by the melting snow and breaking up of the ice had nearly subsided, the Indians came — a hundred or more — into the grove near the house, and prepared for making sugar. Hobson now sent his family to Holderman's grove, where he had obtained permission for them to stay a few days, while he with his household goods started for the Du Page, and again aimed to take up his night's lodging at the Frenchman's cabin But the traveling was bad, and his progress slow. Late in the afternoon he got "stalled" in a slough. Taking off his boots and stockings, in order to keep them dry, he waded through on foot, and with great effort succeeded in getting his team through, his clothes the while were wet and freezing.

It being by this time quite dark, and fearing to proceed further, lest he should again be "stalled," there was no other chance than to spend the night upon the open prairie. And having some bedding in the wagon, he made out to pass the night without freezing. In the morning he reached the Frenchman's cabin, where he breakfasted. The next night found him at the Spring Brook, just west of the Du Page river, but it was so dark that he did not venture to cross it, and accordingly camped out again. Here the grass was long, and making his bed upon the ground, he passed the night very comfortably, and the next morning reached his destination. Mr. Scott advised him to bring his family to his place, and let them remain until he could build his cabin. He accordingly did so, and in a few days their own cabin was ready for their reception.

In April Mr. Hobson went again to Ox Bow Prairie for his wagon, taking with him two yoke of cattle, and bringing back some seed corn, and potatoes. His cattle were so poor and weak that he was often obliged to carry the corn and potatoes on his back, the team being hardly able to draw the empty wagon. The Spring and Summer were cold, wet and consequently unfavorable to crops. But little was raised during that year.

Other settlers, whose names have been given, soon located in different parts of the town. The Naper settlement extended into this town, and the pioneer reminiscences contains an account of the settlers here, up to the close of the Black Hawk war.

This town embraces an area of thirty-six square miles, and is bounded by Milton on the north, by Will county on the south, by Downer's grove on the east, and by Naperville on the west. The surface consists chiefly of rolling prairie, interspersed with groves of fine growing timber. This town was formerly called DU PAGE, a name derived from the river, both forks of which run through it, but there being a town in Will county of the same name, it was organized in 1850, under the name of Lisle, in honor of the late S. Lisle Smith, of Chicago.

That part of the village of Naperville which lies in this town includes the county buildings and four churches. The grist mill at Hobson's was among the first established in this part of the county. Brick making is carried on to a considerable extent, and the bricks manufactured are of good quality. The clay requires coarse sand to be worked with it, to give it compactness. At the establishment of Mr. E. M. Carpenter 275,000 were made last year. The other manufactures are of minor importance, it being strictly an agricultural town, in which branch of industry it competes successfully with its neighbors.

There are in this town nine school districts, in all of which schools are taught throughout the school year. Teachers of the best ability are usually employed, and rewarded by a fair compensation. The almost universal custom of *rotation* in the employment of instructors for our schools prevails in this town, the summer term being taught by females, and the winter term by males. The schools are attended by 310 scholars. The fund derived from the sale of the school section was $800. It now amounts to $1,011.66. The amount paid to teachers last year was $820, and the amount expended for repairing and building was $1,830.

Several stone quarries have been opened in this town, from which stone is obtained for lime burning and for building purposes. The Naperville and Oswego plank road was laid through the central part of this town. The projectors of this road thought to facilitate the communication between Oswego, Naperville and Chicago, and thereby retain the travel which would otherwise be drawn to the railroad which was being built at the same time.

The road was completed from Chicago to Naperville, but no farther. The project was a failure; the stock was worthless, for people *would* travel by railroad. The material of which the road was constructed is now being torn up and converted to other uses.

The following is a list of officers for the town o Lisle, who have been elected since its organization in 1850:

SUPERVISORS.

1850 — Amasa Morse.
1851 — Jeduthen Hatch.
1852 — John Stanley.
1853 — Lewis Ellsworth.
1854 — H. H. Cody.
1855 — J. C. Hatch,
1856 — A. Morse.
1857 — John Collins.

TOWN CLERKS.

1850 — J. C. Hatch.
1851 — George Roush.
1852 — H. F. Vallette.
1853 — S. M. Skinner.
1854 — H. F. Vallette.
1855 —   "
1856 — R. W. Hunt.
1857 — A. S. Barnard.

OVERSEERS OF POOR.

1850 — John Olney.
1851 —   "
1852 —   "
1853 — W. B. Stewart,
1854 — F. A. Smith.
1855 — John Thompson.
1856 — J. A. Richards.
1857 — John Rahm.

COLLECTORS.

1850 — C. K. W. Howard.	1854 — F. A. Smith.
1851 — F. A. Smith.	1855 — B. F. Hosler.
1852 — "	1856 — J. H. Hobson.
1853 — "	1857 — C. M. Goodrich.

COMMISSIONERS OF HIGHWAYS.

1850 — Joseph Blodgett, John Rahm, Ethan Griswold.	1854 — John Sargent, John Stanley, T. Hilderbrand.
1851 — John Rahm, J. Blodgett, Henry Ingalls.	1855 — John Sargent, F. A. Smith, Henry Ingalls.
1852 — Solomon Mertz, E. Griswold, Joseph Blodgett.	1856 — R. S. Palmer, E. Page, D. C. Stanley.
1853 — A. S. Barnard, R. M. Hunt, R. Puffer.	1857 — S. Mertz, R. S. Palmer, J. A. Ballou.

CONSTABLES.

1850 — F. A. Smith.	1854 — John Graves.
1851 — "	1855 — B. F. Hosler.
1852 — John Graves.	1856 — John H. Hobson.
1853 — "	1857 — "

ASSESSORS.

1850 — Jeduthen Hatch.	1854 — A. B. Chatfield.
1851 — A. B. Chatfield.	1855 — "
1852 — "	1856 — C. H. Goodrich.
1853 — D. M. Green.	1857 — Elijah Root.

JUSTICES OF THE PEACE.

1850 — A. B. Chatfield, George Roush.	1854 — A. B. Chatfield, John J. Kimball.

HISTORY OF THE TOWN OF BLOOMING-DALE.

Silas Meacham, Lyman Meacham, and Harvey Meacham, were the first settlers of this town. They came here together, and clearing away the snow from a spot selected for the purpose, pitched their tents, on the eleventh day of March, 1833. The Indians, who were numerous at that time, were their only neighbors during the first year. There were no settlers nearer than King's grove, on the east branch of the DU PAGE, none on the Chicago and Galena road, and none on Fox river above Green's mill. Their Indian neighbors were generally peaceable and quiet, but filled with all manner of superstitious and *savage* peculiarities. Soon after the settlement commenced, a dog was discovered in the grove hanging from a limb to which it was fastened, with a piece of tobacco tied to each foot. The settlers afterward learned from Lawton, an Indian trader, that the Indians had had some bad luck, and the dog was offered as a sacrifice.

The grove was known among the Indians as Penneack grove, and received its name from a root found in it, resembling the potato. It grew in such abundance, that the Indians came for it, and carried it away to their camps, in sacks, on their ponies.

The Indians were generally trusty, and on the whole proved themselves good neighbors. The settlers placed great confidence in them. They frequently came to the settlement to borrow, and were always prompt in returning, thereby offering an example which many "white folks" think it too much trouble to follow in all cases. Harvey Meacham once loaned his valuable rifle to one of them for several days, on the promise that he would return it at a certain time ; the Indian, faithful to his word, brought it back on the appointed day.

The wife of Lyman Meacham died in the fall of 1833. Her coffin was made of boards taken from a wagon box which was brought from the east. The next death in the settlement was that of a young mechanic, who came into the town with Major Skinner, in 1834. He was buried in a coffin made of plank, split from a log in the grove.

A small addition to the settlement was made in 1834. Among the settlers of that year were H. Woodworth, N. Stevens, D. Bangs, Elias Maynard, and Major Skinner. The Meacham brothers, during the first year, built a log house for each of their families, broke and planted forty acres of prairie, and fenced it in, to secure it from their stock which grazed upon the open fields. At the end of the year 1834, the settlement had increased to twelve or fifteen families. Many trials, incident to the settlers of a new country, were experienced by these first pioneers. We are informed by one of them, that it was no uncommon thing for a man to take his plow share and mould board, weighing some sixty pounds, upon his back and trudge away to Chicago, a distance of twenty-four miles, to get it sharpened.

The precinct of Cook county, in which this settlement was included, extended over a large part, if not all of Cook county, west of the O'Plain river.

The first election in this precinct was held at Elk grove, eight miles north east of Bloomingdale. Lyman Meacham was elected justice of the peace. The first path master went as far south as Warrenville, ten miles distant, to warn out the settlers on the highway to perform their road labor. The claim difficulty to which allusion has been made, occurred in this town. It is thought that no correct history of the horrid transaction has ever appeared. The statement of this affair, given in the life of George W. Green, the banker, who committed suicide in the Chicago jail, is very erroneous. The compilers have been at considerable pains to obtain a brief, and as they believe, an impartial account of the transaction, which is commonly known as

THE KENT TRAGEDY.

In the year 1835, or thereabouts, Ebenezer Peck bought the undivided half of Dr. Meacham's claim. While they held it jointly, they leased it to Milton Kent. Before the lease expired, Dr. Meacham sold his half to Mr. Peck, and moved to the O'Plain river, previous to any difficulty with Kent. The trouble respecting the claim commenced soon after Mr. Peck became the sole owner. Mr. Kent's lease expired in the spring of 1837, and the claim was sold to George W. Green, of Chicago, who came on to occupy it, but Mr. Kent would not allow him to take possession; whereupon, a suit at law was brought, which after several years' litigation, resulted in giving Green a title to the whole property. In the mean time, Mr. Kent

had built a house and barn suited to the business of
tavern keeping, near the east end of the claim, and
upon a piece of land which *he and his friends said*,
Dr. Meacham gave him for a tavern stand. Near the
first of March 1840, Mr. Green and family, accompanied by Daniel M. Green, the sheriff of DU PAGE
County, came on to the ground and demanded the
possession of the entire premises, tavern stand included.
Mr. Kent was very unwilling to go, but notwithstanding his reluctance, he was forced to remove his household effects from the house he had built, and quit the
premises on which he had invested all he had. His
furniture was removed to a shanty which had been
hastily constructed of boards upon the claim, at a little
distance from the house. The sheriff notified him to
leave the claim immediately; but at the old man's
earnest request that he might remain over the Sabbath,
it being then Saturday night, it was provided that he
could do so upon the condition that he would depart
early on Monday.

Old Mr. Kent was a man of iron will, and determined still to have the property, and stake everything
on the effort, preferring even death itself, to being
conquered. After preparing a quit claim deed, the
following plan, as revealed by those concerned in it,
was adopted.

The old man, accompanied by his son, son-in-law,
a friend, who afterwards married into the family, and
a hired man, making five in all, were to go to the
house of Mr. Green late on Sunday evening, decoy
him to the door, seize him, carry him off and force him
to sign the deed. When the time arrived they went

to the house. Four of the number were on foot, and took their station at the side of the door, to seize Green when he came out, while the fourth, who was on horseback, rode up in front of the house and called loudly for Mr. Green; but, instead of going to the door, Mr. Green answered him through the window of the room in which he was sleeping. The horseman told him that he wished to stop there over night, to which Mr. Green replied that the house was no longer a tavern; that he could obtain lodging a little further on. He had scarcely said this when the outside door was broken in with a loud crash. In an instant the four men who had been stationed at the door appeared in his room. He had prepared himself with arms for his defense, should he be molested, and seizing his rifle, fired in the direction of the assaulters. The ball passed through the collar of old Mr. Kent's coat, and escaped through the window frame. He then snapped his pistol, the muzzle being against the breast of one of his assailants, but the collar of his coat caught in the lock in some way, and it missed fire.

The room was very dark, and, therefore, Green had the better chance to defend himself. In entering the room a table of dishes was overturned, and two of the number sprang upon the bed, seizing Mrs. Green, whom they mistook for her husband. Finding their mistake, they left her unharmed, and went to the assistance of their comrades. In the meantime, Green seized a large butcher knife, and commenced making desperate thrusts with it at all who came in his way. A son of Mr. Kent succeeded, at length, in grasping Green tightly around the body, in such a manner as to give

him but little use of his arms; but he soon regretted
his rashness, for it was not long before he felt the
sharp point of the knife entering his back, and making
an awful wound.   He cried murder, implored Green
to spare his life, and his comrades to come to his
assistance.

Old Mr. Kent advanced, and was about to lay hold
of Green, when he (Green) drew the knife from the
body of the young man, and struck the old man a
mortal blow under the left arm, at which he raised
his hands, gave a dying shriek, left the room unob-
served, walked a few paces from the door, and fell to
the ground dead.

Young Kent was now released from Green's grasp,
and, notwithstanding he had received, as he supposed,
a mortal wound, he still determined to conquer, and
the party rallied, with all their strength, to make one
more effort to secure Green.   A furious onslaught
ensued, and Green was at last overpowered, although
he fought desperately.   He was knocked down, and
beaten with merciless severity upon the head with a
horse pistol, and afterward taken, in a senseless condition, from the floor and carried, without clothing,
save his shirt, across the fields to the shanty.   When
he had recovered his senses, he was there required to
sign the paper, and the young man whom he had so
severely wounded with the knife remarked that " he
must do it d—n quick, too, for he wanted to see it
done before he died, and his boots were then over-
flowing with blood."   Expecting that his life would
be taken in any event, Green signed the papers in
presence of the daughters, and then importuned them

to let him die at once, upon which he was taken back across the field, and left, in an almost helpless state, near his house, which he succeeded in reaching soon after.

Mrs. Green, after witnessing the brutal treatment of her husband, and being left alone in the house, suffered the most intense alarm, supposing he would be killed, and that a similar fate awaited herself. She stood at the door crying murder, in a voice not above a whisper. The death of old Mr. Kent was not known to his son until after the papers were signed.

Consternation filled the minds of the settlers at such a tragedy transpiring in their midst. A sight never to be forgotten was the lifeless body of that old man, as it lay there upon the ground, his hair white like the frost of winter gathering around his icy temples, and ruffled by the passing breeze, as it moaned among the branches of the grove. His countenance was fresh as though life yet lingered in his veins, but his limbs were stiff and cold in death.

Green delivered himself up to the proper authority, and went before the grand jury of Du Page County, confessed the crime he had committed, and was discharged. Writs were issued for the arrest of Lorenzo Kent and others, concerned in the tragic affair. Kent was arrested, and while too ill, as was supposed, to be removed, fled out of the State. The family were scattered, and have never been united since in that hallowed relation. Their head being removed, and themselves being left without a home, they have been compelled to wander from the scenes of their early attachment, at the mercy of an uncharitable world.

Mr. Green remained in the place some three years,
but was in constant fear of his life. He never left his
house without being armed, and always slept with
weapons within his reach. The opinion prevailed
among the settlers that he was a dangerous person,
and few tears were shed when he sold his claim and
left the neighborhood. His subsequent career of
crime, which terminated in self-destruction, is familiar
to all. He removed to Chicago, where he amassed
considerable wealth in the banking business. In 1855
he was convicted of the crime of murder, in poisoning
his wife, and lodged in the Chicago jail. Soon after
his conviction, and while confined in jail, he was found
dead in his cell, having taken his own life rather than
undergo the execution of his sentence. Thus, we
have endeavored to present a brief and impartial statement of the Kent affair, about which so much has
been said and written. This, as we have already in-
timated, was the only serious claim difficulty in this
county; but volumes might be filled with the most
thrilling tales of conflict between settlers, respecting
their claims, in other parts of the west. Were government to survey its lands before they are settled upon,
a portion, at least, of the difficulties now incident to
new settlements would be avoided.

Bloomingdale is not excelled by any of its sister
towns in healthfulness of climate, fertility of soil,
beauty of scenery, variety of products, nor in attention
to agriculture. Meacham's grove is in this town, and
embraces about 1,200 acres of fine timber. The trail
made by Gen. Scott's army, in passing from Fort
Dearborn to the Mississippi, is about a mile and a half

south of the grove. The trail was visible when the first settlers came, and has always been known as the army trail road. The source of the east branch of the Du Page river is from low land about half a mile south of the grove. The west branch rises in a slough, a few rods in width, situated near the north east corner of the town of Wayne. The town is well watered by springs and small streams, it having but one stream of any size. A branch of Salt creek runs in an easterly direction through the town, uniting with the main branch at Duncklee's grove, in the town of Addison. This stream furnishes water power at some seasons, and a saw mill has been erected upon it.

The village of Bloomingdale contains about thirty dwelling houses, one hotel, 5 factories, 2 stores, and three churches. The Baptist society was organized in March, 1841, through the instrumentality of Rev. Joel Wheeler and Rev. A. W. Button. There were at first seventeen members, among whom were Noah Stevens, Ephraim Kettle, Asa Dudley, F. R. Stevens, Orange Kent, J. D. Kinne, Philo Nobles, Silas Farr, and William Farr.

For several years the society was without a settled minister, during which time preaching was sustained by Rev. Joel Wheeler, Rev. A. W. Button, Rev. Mr. Smith, Rev. Mr. Edwards, and Rev. Mr. Dickens. The first settled minister was Rev. P. Taylor, who became pastor of the church in 1848, and continued until 1855. He was succeeded by Rev. J. H. Worrell, the present pastor, in 1855.

There have been 204 members of this church since its organization. Seventy-eight have been dismissed,

and four only have died during their membership.
The Society now numbers 126 resident members.
There is a Sabbath school of 40 scholars connected
with this church, having a library of 450 volumes.
The present house of worship was built in 1848.

The Congregational Church was organized in August, 1840, by Rev. D. Rockwell, assisted by Rev. F.
Bascomb. W. Dodge, A. Buck, Elijah Hough, A.
Hills, E. Thayer, C. H. Meacham, and J. P. Yalding,
were among the first members. Rev. D. Rockwell
was ordained in 1840, and continued as pastor until
1842. The following are the names of pastors since
that time :

1842 — Rev. L. Parker.	1850 — Rev. N. Shapley.
1843 — " H. Colton.	1851 — " L. Parker.
1844 — " B. W. Reynolds.	1854 — " D. Chapman. [tor.
1846 — " L. Parker.	1855 — " H. Judd, present pas-

There have been 203 members in all, of whom
eleven have died during their membership. There
are now 93 resident members. The Sabbath school
has about 50 scholars, and a library of 300 volumes.
The church of this Society was built in 1851, and
dedicated June 13th, 1852.

The Methodist Society of this town is in a prosperous condition, being at present supplied with preachers
from the Naperville circuit.

There are nine school districts in this town, eight of
which have school houses. The school fund derived
from sale of land was $1,028. It is now $1,425.
There were 325 scholars in attendance during the past
year. Trustees, Captain E. Kinne, H. Barnes, H. S.
Hills. Treasurer, S. P. Sedgwick.

The first town meeting in Bloomingdale was held at the school house, in the village, on Tuesday, the 2d day of April, 1850. We give below the names of town officers since the adoption of the township organization law :

SUPERVISORS :

1850 — Erasmas O. Hills.	1854 — John G. Yearick,
1851 — Erasmas O. Hills.	1855 — Daniel F. Deibert.
1852 — H. B. Hills.	1856 — Horace Barnes.
1853 — Cyrus H. Meacham.	1857 — Cyrus H. Meacham.

TOWN CLERKS :

1850 — Myron C. Dudley.	1854 — H. B. Hills.
1851 — Asa W. Spitzer.	1855 — H. B. Hills.
1852 — M. C. Dudley.	1856 — H. B. Hills.
1853 — M. C. Dudley.	1857 — H. B. Hills.

JUSTICES OF THE PEACE :

1850 — C. H. Meacham,	1854 — S. P. Sedgwick,
H. Bronson Hills.	James Vint.
1851 — Hiram Goodwin.	

CONSTABLES :

1850 — Huet O. Hills,	1853 — James Vint.
L. E. Reed.	1854 — S. O. Pepper.
1851 — H. O. Hills.	1855 — S. O. Pepper.
1852 — J. G. Yearick.	1856 — Geo F. Deibert.

COMMISSIONERS OF HIGHWAYS :

1850 — S. H. Dinsmore,	1852 — Rowland Rathbun,
J. H. Kelsey,	James Vint,
James Vint.	H. Benjamin,
1851 — D. S. Meacham,	1853 — J. Barnes,
J. Hathorn,	R. Rathbun,
S. C. McDowel.	J. N. Nind.

7

COMMISSIONERS OF HIGHWAYS—CONTINUED:

1854 — L. E. Landon,   1856 — Asa Clark,
       J. Barnes,   Berlin Godfrey,
       J. N. Nind.   J. A. Kelsey.
1855 — D. F. Deibert,   1857 — J. V. McGraw,
       Milton Smith,   Alfred Rich,
       B. C. Pendleton.   Pierce Driscol.

ASSESSORS:

1850 — Jonathan Barnes.   1854 — Asa Dudley.
1851 — H. H. Coe.   1855 — D. S. McGraw.
1852 — C. H. Meacham.   1856 — Milton Smith.
1853 — H. Benjamin.   1857 — W. K. Patrick.

OVERSEERS OF THE POOR:

1850 — L. E. Landon.   1854 — Allen Hills.
1851 — Calvin Muzzy.   1855 — Allen Hills.
1852 — H. Meacham.   1856 — Levi H. Kinne.
1853 — Allen Hills.   1857 — Levi H. Kinne.

COLLECTORS:

1850 — H. O. Hills.   1854 — S. O. Pepper.
1851 — H. O. Hills.   1855 — S. O. Pepper.
1852 — J. G. Yearick.   1856 — Asa Dudley.
1853 — James Vint.   1857 — Asa Dudley.

HISTORY OF THE TOWN OF ADDISON.

THE settlement of this town began in 1834. The first inhabitants were Ebenezer Duncklee and Hezekiah Duncklee, from Hillsborough, N. H., and Mason Smith, from Potsdam, N. Y. They left Potsdam on the 13th of August, 1833, and arrived at Chicago on the 3d of September, traveling by land across Michigan and Northern Indiana. Leaving Chicago on the 8th of September, they followed the trail of Gen. Scott's army, which had preceded them, to the Des Plaines river, where they camped for the night, near a party of 300 Indians. On the following day, they proceeded along the trail as far as the south line of Addison. Here they found a grave, which was supposed to be that of a soldier in Gen. Scott's army. The grave was on the west bank of Salt creek. On the opposite bank, near what is now called Grey's grove, were the remains of the army encampment. Some of the tent posts were still standing. Upon examination, it was found that the waters of the creek were not salt, as they had supposed. The stream received its name from this circumstance: A hoosier team, loaded with salt, became "stalled" while fording it, and the driver was obliged to lighten his load by rolling several barrels into the water. The party left the creek at 5 o'clock, and pursued the trail. Soon after dark they discovered a light, which seemed at no great distance. One of the company set out in advance, hoping to reach it, but after making a circuit through the tall prairie grass, he came upon his comrades near the place from which he started — and the party camped for the night among the prairie grass and flowers. Their slumbers were somewhat disturbed by the prairie wolves, which howled most hideously about them during a greater part of the night; but wearied by their long marches, they rested full as well as could be expected under the circumstances. On the following day they reached Meacham's grove, where they found three settlers by the name of Meacham. Here they obtained some instruction in the arts of border life. They learned how to make their claims, how to construct cabins, and how to manufacture their beds. From this place they proceeded to Elk grove, and thence along the west bank of Salt creek to Duncklee's grove, and camped for the night on the spot where the house of H. D. Fisher now stands.

On the 12th day of September they took a northern direction through the timber, and made their claims near the north end of the grove. The timber claims were made by marking trees, and the prairie claims by plowing a furrow entirely around each. Immediate preparations were made for the erection of a *house*. The ground was leveled with a hoe, and prairie grass, which was cut with an ax, was spread upon it for beds. A tent was made of cotton cloth, and here they lived for half a month, until their cabin could be completed. The sides of the new cabin were formed of logs, drawn together by the pony — an important member of the company, of whom honorable mention is hereafter made — the floor was formed of split logs, and the roof of oak shingles. The family of E. Duncklee arrived in August, 1834. The 18th day of June, 1835, was the date of the birth of the first white child in the town. Three barrels of frozen apples were planted by Mr. Duncklee in the spring of 1836, from which nearly all the region has been supplied with fruit trees. He sold from his own orchard, in 1855, upward of $600 worth of fruit. There is a cotton-wood tree standing in his yard which sprang from seed sown in 1837, and measures five feet two inches in circumference, at a height of fourteen inches from the ground.

The following table gives the names of the early settlers, the date of settlement, and the state or country from which they emigrated:

NAMES.	YEAR.	WHERE FROM.
Hezekiah Duncklee	1834	N. H.
Mason Smith	"	"
E. Duncklee	1835	"
A. Ingals	1834	Mass.
C. Fisher	"	Germany.
H. Smith, sen	1835	"
Geo. Rouse	"	N. Y.
E. Lester	"	"
M. Lester	"	"
F. Lester	"	"
D. Lester	"	"
J. F. Franzen	1836	Germany.
B. Kaler	"	"
D. S. Dunning	"	N. Y.
D. Gray	1834	Germany.
F. Gray	"	"
H. D. Fisher	1836	"
H. Smith, jun	1835	"
F. Smith	"	"
T. Thomson	1834	"
Lewis Smith	1835	"
H. Rotermund	1837	"
F. Kragie	"	"
F. Stainkle	"	"
J. Bertman	1836	"
S. D. Pierce	"	N. Y.
C. W. Martin	"	"
W. Boske	1835	Germany.
B. F. Fillmore	1836	Vermont.
Edwin Pierce	1837	N. Y.

This is strictly an agricultural town. The first attempt at farming, of which the writer has any account, was in the fall of 1834. Mason Smith and Hezekiah Duncklee cut and stacked a few tons of hay near Salt creek, to keep a small pony, which was their joint possession, and which had brought them all the way from Detroit. Their stack was completed after several days' hard labor, and they were advised to burn the grass for several rods around it, in order to protect it from the annual fires set by the Indians. Being unacquainted with the business, they set the fire too near, and not only burned up the grass about it, but the whole stack was consumed, leaving the pony destitute of a winter's allowance. Winter came on, and having no hay, they turned him into the grove, where he lived and prospered until the opening of spring. The land in this town came into market in 1842, having been surveyed the previous year. When the first settlers came into the town, the land being unsurveyed, each made what was termed a claim, by staking or surrounding with a furrow as much land as he thought he would be able to pay for, when it should come into market. The usual quantity claimed was 160 acres; some, however, claimed more, and some less than that amount. There were some conflicting claims; but these difficulties were generally settled when the land was sold, by the one having the largest portion of the disputed claim buying the whole, and then re-deeding to each holder his proportion. In this way all obtained their lands as claimed, without regard to government lines. There are three groves of thrifty growing timber in this town. Duncklee's grove lies on the east bank and along the Salt creek. It is about three miles in length, and half a mile in width. Grey's grove lies also on the east branch of Salt creek, and contains about 100 acres. Kaler's grove, though smaller, affords considerable fuel and timber. The balance of the lands of this town is chiefly flat prairie. The soil is from two to two and one-half feet in depth, with a subsoil of clay. It produces good spring wheat, oats, corn, potatoes, etc. Winter wheat generally kills out in the spring, by alternate freezing and thawing. The greater part of the hay is made from prairie grass, which grows luxuriantly on the creek bottoms, and on the low ground. Clover, timothy and herdsgrass do well, but require manure to neutralize the alkalies in the land. The lands produce an average of about twenty bushels of spring wheat, forty bushels of oats, forty bushels of corn, and one hundred bushels of potatoes to the acre.

The price of farms in this town varies according to their improvement. The minimum value is $25 per acre, and the maximum $50.

The school section of this town sold for $800, which has been increased, by addition of interest from time to time, to $1,300. There are eight school districts in the town, six of which are provided with good school buildings. There are three German schools taught. Henry Bartling is the post master in the south part of the town, and S. D. Pierce at Sagone, in the north part. There are three churches, two establishments for the manufacture of brick, one grist mill, one carriage shop, one cabinet shop, four stores, two boot and shoe shops, and two blacksmith shops in the town. The Lutherans have a large society, and worship in a house built for their own accommodation. The present pastor is Rev. E. A. Brauer.

The German Methodist society of this town is also large. It has a house of worship, and the pulpit is regularly supplied by a settled pastor. The present pastor of this church is Rev. U. Macklin.

This town has been visited with several violent and destructive storms within a few years past, the effects of which were also experienced in other parts of the county, and through the kindness of Mr. M. L. Dunlap, Esq., we are enabled to place some account of them before our readers. The following communication was published in the Chicago *Democrat*, of June 13, 1847:

THE HAIL STORM.

"This part of the country was yesterday visited with one of the severest storms of rain and hail that I have ever witnessed — the country is completely inundated. The morning was cloudy, with wind from the south, occasionally shifting to the southwest; during the forenoon, the clouds gave the appearance of good weather. At 7 A. M. the barometer stood at 29.50 inches, and thermometer at 68°. At 12 o'clock the latter had risen to 77°, and the former had fallen to 28.40 inches. At this time a thunder shower was rolling up its black masses from the northwest, and at 1 o'clock it burst upon us with full force, attended with large quantities of hail of icy firmness. The mass of hail stones would average three-eights of an inch in diameter, while many specimens picked up measured over one and a half inches in circumference.

Several lighter showers followed, with wind from

the southeast; and at 4 o'clock a heavy shower presented itself in the north, extending itself south and east, with wind from the east. In a few minutes the wind suddenly shifted to the north, when the rain commenced falling in torrents, completely shutting out the view. The rain partially abated, when the hail commenced pouring down at a fearful rate, the average size of the hail stones being half an inch in diameter, while many of them would measure over three inches in circumference, being an aggregation of hail stones cemented together—perfect ragged lumps of ice. The barometer fell to 28.30 inches, and thermometer to 59°; after the storm the latter rose to 67°, and the former to 28.40 inches. There was but little wind during the falling of the hail.

This morning the houses, gardens and fields were a dismal sight. Nearly all the glass is out of the windows on the north sides of the houses, the young fruit is stripped from the trees, buds and grafts of this year's growth are broken off, and the field crops are more than half destroyed. The damage to our farms in this part of the county will be severely felt." Here is another dated July 15th, 1854.

A DESTRUCTIVE STORM.

"We turn aside from our usual articles on culture, to record one of the most destructive hail storms within our knowledge. It occurred about 5 o'clock P. M., Thursday, the 13th instant. Commencing in the town of Bloomingdale, Du Page County, and passing through Addison in the same county, thence into Cook county through the north part of Leyden,

7*

the south part of Elk grove and Maine, thence through
Niles to the lake. . Its track of greatest destruction
was about a mile in width, though the hail fell in torrents, doing more or less damage for a mile on each
side of this line. The entire crops of grain and potatoes are completely broken down and ruined; the
grass has fared little better, being badly injured and
much of it not worth cutting. The corn is completely
stripped of its leaves, and mostly broken off near the
ground. Fruit and shade trees are nearly defoliated,
badly bruised, and in many cases large stripes of bark
knocked off. At the house of I. Knowles, in Addison,
a pile of hail stones accumulated in an angle of the
building three feet deep, and at 5 o'clock next day,
hail stones were measured from this pile from three
to five inches in circumference. The trees on this
farm are mostly stripped of their bark.

All the windows on the south and west sides of the
houses had the glass broken. Cattle ran bellowing
through the fields—horses broke from their fastenings
and ran with whatever was fast to them. The ten
minutes the hail was falling, were of fearful grandeur,
alarm and rapid destruction. The dark mass of cloud
streaked with the lurid lightning—the roaring of the
hail like the pouring out of a thousand torrents might
well inspire terror and dismay. In a few short minutes the hopes of the husbandman were gone; the
broad ears of beautiful waving grain fast ripening for
the reaper, and which were destined to feed and clothe
those he held most dear, were utterly ruined and pros-
trated before him. Think you, gentle reader, that no
tears coursed down the sun-burnt cheeks of those

hardy sons of toil, to see their cherished hopes thus swept away, themselves, teams and farm implements turned out nearly idle for the remainder of the season; and the hopes of their families resting on their daily labor, or the prospect of a mortgage to carry them forward to another harvest? We know the heart of the farmer is large, and ever open to relieve the unfortunate, and in this case we feel assured that those in the immediate vicinity will extend a helping hand in the way of grass, grain, and labor, not forgetting those garden vegetables so desirable to the health and comfort of a family.

Yesterday we passed over a small portion of the unfortunate tract, and made some figures of the loss, but these embrace only a small portion, and do not include all within the distance passed over, as we prefer to omit the estimate rather than take them from hearsay. In this estimate we have taken, the probable amount of grain, etc., at its market price, after deducting the cost of harvesting and marketing. It is probably much below the ultimate loss in deranging farm operations, and the extra expense of procuring hay and grain for farm use:

Wm. Richardson,	$600	M. Millner,	$500
D. Lester,	600	Mr. Millner,	350
C. Heimsoth,	200	J. & J. Baker,	450
Mr. Bottings,	250	J. Knowls,	600
J. H. Ehle,	400	T. D. Pierce,	500
S. D. Pierce,	900	Messrs. Chesman,	400
A. Ingals,	300	Messrs. Lock,	100
A. Tupp,	100	L. Gary.	300
Mr. Ohlerking,	800	Mrs. Going,	500
F. Turner,	600	B. F. Fillmore,	200
D. S. Dunning,	400	C. W. Martin,	300

C. Schwitzer,..............300	G. Landmair,..............300
F. Teduka,................400	H. Hadkin,................200
Dr. E. Smith,............200	J. Fennemore, ...900
Lewis Lester,..............100	T. B. Cochran,............600
D. Clark, jr.,..............500	

This list, imperfect as it is, shows a large loss for a small neighborhood in a rural district, and nearly all within the delivery of the Sagone post office, in the town of Addison. The south margin of the storm passed over Dunlap's nursery, in the town of Leyden, injuring the young grafts and knocking off fruit from the specimen grounds, which is to be regretted, as many varieties were fruiting for the first time, by which their correctness of nomenclature would have been decided. Such large quantities of decaying vegetable matter, now sweltering in a summer sun, cannot have otherwise than a deleterious effect on the health of families residing on this track of desolation."

Under the township organization law, the first town election took place in Addison, in April, 1850. The following list includes the names of town officers since that time:

SUPERVISOR:

1850 — S. D. Pierce.	1854 — J. Wakeman.
1851 — P. Northrop.	1855 — H. D. Fisher.
1852 — J. Pierce.	1856 — "
1853 — E. Lester.	1857 — "

TOWN CLERK:

1850 — P. Northrop.	1854 — B. F. Fillmore.
1851 — B. F. Fillmore.	1855 — "
1852 — "	1856 — "
1853 — "	1857 — H. Bartling.

ASSESSOR :

1850 — H. Rotermuud.   1854 — S. D. Pierce.
1851 —   "   1855 — N. Sadler.
1852 — L. Barnum.   1856 — J. A. Kinne.
1853 — S. D. Pierce.   1857 — S. D. Pierce.

CONSTABLE :

1850 — W. Rotermund,   1854 — S. D. Pierce.
  "   S. D. Pierce.   1855 — L. Rust,
1851 —   "   "   J. Pierce.
1852 —   "   1856 —   "
1853 —   "   1857 — G. Schneider.

COLLECTOR :

1850 — W. Rotermund.   1854 — L. Rotermund.
1851 —   "   1855 — L. Rust.
1852 — T. E. Lester.   1856 —   "
1853 — L. Rotermund.   1857 — T. Smith.

JUSTICE OF THE PEACE :

1850 — S. D. Pierce,   H. D. Fisher.
    Peter Northrup.   1854 —   "
1851 —   "   1855 —   "
1852 —   "   1856 —   "
1853 — S. D. Pierce,   1857 —   "

HISTORY OF THE TOWN OF WINFIELD.

This town was settled in 1832 by Erastus and Jude P. Gary. They came in just after the close of the Black Hawk war, and settled in the east part of the town. Among the settlers of 1834 were Messrs. M. Griswold, J. M. Warren, J. S. P. Lord, A. Churchill, Alvah Fowler, Ira Herrick, and Ezra Galusha. The town is six miles square; is well supplied with wood and timber; is watered by the Du Page and several smaller streams; has a productive soil and healthy climate; and is now rapidly increasing in wealth and population.

There are in the town three pleasant villages, three churches, one academy, one grist mill, two saw mills, twelve stores, ten factories, three post offices, two railroad stations, and a population of about 1,600.

Of the three villages — Warrenville, Winfield and Turner — Warrenville was first settled. The first house was built by Col. J. M. Warren in 1834. There are now in the village a Baptist church, an incorporated academy, a grist mill, a saw mill, three blacksmith shops, two dry goods stores, one drug store, a post office, two wagon shops, a hotel, and about 250 inhabitants. The village is pleasantly situated on the west fork of the Du Page river, three miles from Winfield station, on the G. & C. U. railroad.

The first efforts toward establishing a religious organization in Winfield were commenced at this place by a few members of the Du Page Baptist church, as early as 1834. February 4th, 1836, preparatory measures were taken to organize a society. At a meeting held at that time, after some discussion, the following preamble and resolutions were adopted: " *Whereas*, in the providence of God, we are located in this part of God's moral vineyard, and at a considerable distance from our mother church, or any other church of the same faith and order: *Resolved*, That we organize ourselves into a regular Baptist church, to be located at Warrenville, and to be called the Second Du Page Baptist church: *Resolved*, That we send letters to sister churches, inviting them to send their pastors and deacons, for the purpose of giving us fellowship as a sister church."

On the 23d of February the society met at Warrenville for the purpose of organizing, and the following churches were represented: First Baptist church of Chicago, by Elder J. T. Hinton and Deacon Jonson; First Church of Du Page, by Elder A. B. Hubbard and Judge Wilson.

The council was duly organized by the appointment of Judge Wilson moderator, and A. E. Carpenter scribe. The articles of faith, and practice and covenant, were then presented to the council, with the names of the members proposing to be recognized. Sixteen members were present, and it was resolved by the council: "That we recognize these members as a regular Baptist church." The services of recognition then took place. A sermon was preached by Elder J. T. Hinton, and the right hand of fellowship was given and a prayer offered by Elder Hubbard. The following are the names of the members recognized:

A. E. Carpenter, Sarah Carpenter, Manus Griswold, Sophia Griswold, Alfred Churchill, Susannah Churchill, J. S. P. Lord, Mary Lord, Nancy Warren, Philinda Warren, Joseph Fish.

Several ministers took a deep interest at an early day in this branch of Zion. Among them was Elder Ashley, whose name is embalmed in the hearts of the pious in this part of the Lord's vineyard. He was with this church through several precious revivals, and was the means, in the hand of God, of bringing many from darkness to light. The first pastor of this society was Elder L. B. King. He has been succeeded by Elders A. B. Hubbard, Joel Wheeler, A. J. Joslyn, A. Taylor, Joel Wheeler, S. F. Holt, —— Freeman, and H. Westcott, the present pastor, who recently came to this state from New Jersey. The society worshipped in a private house for some time in its early history, there being no school house in or about Warrenville, in which to hold its meetings. The first school house built here was occupied by the church until the old church building was purchased of Col. Warren and fitted up for the use of the society. A large and handsome church edifice is now in process of erection. The corner stone was laid July 22d, 1857. The ceremonies were conducted by Rev. Dr. Howard and Rev. Mr. Boyd, of Chicago; Rev. Mr. Raymond and Rev. Mr. Estee, of Aurora; Rev. J. H. Worrell, of Bloomingdale; Rev. E. Barker, of Naperville; and Rev. H. Westcott, pastor. The house is 35 feet by 66, surmounted with a beautiful spire. The cost of building, including bell and fixtures, is estimated at between four and five thousand dollars. Connected with this church are a Sabbath school of fifty scholars, and two interesting bible classes. There are now belonging to this church fifty members.

A Presbyterian church was organized in the west part of the town in 1836, by Rev. Mr. Clark, missionary, with seven members. Rev. Washington Wilcox commenced preaching at the Big Woods in 1836, and continued as their circuit preacher until 1839. In June, 1839, the Big Woods church was completed, having been built by the united efforts of the Congregational, Baptist, and Methodist societies, who have occupied it alternately since that time. The Rev. Mr. Baxter officiates at this time as the Congregational pastor, and Rev. H. Westcott as the Baptist pastor. There are at present about eight Baptist members, and about the same number of Congregational members.

From 1836 to 1844, the house of John Warne was occupied as a place of worship by the Episcopal Methodists living on the east side of the Big Woods. That branch of the society now worships in the Big Woods church.

There is a small settlement at Gary's mill, near the centre of the town. The first settler here was Rev. Charles Gary, who came in 1837. The saw mill was erected in that year. A society of Methodists, seven in number, was formed here under the labors of Rev. W. Wilcox, in 1837, since which time the society has been supplied with preachers appointed to labor on the Naperville circuit. There are at present twenty resident members — many of the members residing in other towns having withdrawn and formed new classes. The Sabbath school of this society was commenced in

1838. It now numbers 46 scholars, and has a library of between two and three hundred volumes. The original members of this society were Angus Ross, Elizabeth Ross, Erastus Gary, J. P. Gary, Orinda Gary, Samuel Arnold, and Mrs. Arnold.

There are 10 and 68-100 miles of railroad in this town, on which the villages of Winfield, or Fredericksburg, and Turner are situated. The first building at Winfield was erected by John Hodges, in 1849, and occupied for several-years as the depot of the G. & C. U. Railroad. This station is the nearest point on the railroad to Naperville, and hence its freight business is large. A greater amount of tonnage is sent from this place than from any other station in the county. The present station house was built in 1854. There are in the place three stores, an extensive lumber yard, owned by Mr. John Collins, several manufactories, and a brewery.

The following account of the village of Turner has been furnished by Dr. J. McConnell, and rather than run the risk of marring it by any rude touches of our own pen, we insert it *verbatim*.

"The village of Turner is situated in a healthy region, some thirty miles west of Chicago. It is the centre of a rich and fertile plain, gently undulating, and beautifully interspersed with luxuriant groves and verdant prairie, with here and there the farmer's home rising up as monuments of industry and beacons of domestic peace. It is at the junction of four railroads, viz.: the Galena & Chicago Union Railroad, running from this point to Galena, Ill., and Dubuque, Iowa; the Chicago Iowa & Nebraska Railroad, running direct to Nebraska, and crossing the Mississippi at Fulton, Ill., and Clinton, Iowa ; and the St. Charles Railroad running to St. Charles.

The first house within the limits of this village was built by Capt. Alonzo Harvey, who bought the claim covering the present village site, and during the time of his residence in said house, his daughter Lois was born, being the first white person born on said grounds. But the Captain soon tired of farming, and sold his claim. He is now a prominent citizen of Chicago, where his daughter Lois, of rare beauty, now at the age of sweet sixteen, mingles a welcome guest in the first circles of society.

The government title to said claim was partly secured in the name of Winslow, and partly in the name of Stickney, after which the most of it fell into the hands of Hon J. B. Turner, the heirs of Mr. Winslow, and Dea. J. McConnell. But no thoughts of a village at this point were entertained by any of the inhabitants until the Galena & Chicago Union Railroad Company commenced to run a branch of their road from this place to Fulton, which branch is now the Chicago, Iowa & Nebraska Railroad. In fact, no effort to build up a village was attempted till the spring of 1856, when Hon. J. B. Turner platted and recorded, according to the statutes of the state, some forty acres, to which C. W. Winslow, Esq., added twenty acres. In the summer following, Deacon J. McConnell made an addition of seventy acres of the most desirable business and dwellings lots in said town. Since which time, there have been sold to actual settlers, about thirty lots, some of which have already been built upon, and upon others, buildings are now being constructed. Within the same time, from a farm adjoining said village (owned by G. W. Eastman,) have been sold about fifteen acres, in lots, ranging from one to two acres, for residences, and though our village now numbers only about five hundred souls, it is a place of vast business energy and active life.

We have recently had an extensive variety store established here, of which Williams & West are the proprietors. They sell their extensive stock at Chicago prices, and are about building an extensive store and storehouse on Depot street, extending across to the railroad track. W. S. Atchinson is also building a large store, for a wholesale and retail boot and shore business.

With all our railroad facilities, this is a choice location to head off large Chicago jobbing houses. Dr. Hall is also building a store for the drug business. J. McDonald has also a large store and storehouse, and deals extensively in dry goods, groceries, hardware and agricultural implements. He also pays cash for all the farmer has to sell, and to show the increase in his business, I give the following statistics : In 1853, when he commenced buying grain, his receipts were only 1200 bushels; in 1854, 3000 bushels; and in 1855 they reached over 30,000 bushels; with a steady increase ever since, together with a trade in butter, lard, pork and wool, to compare.

We have also a large and commodious hotel, of which Messrs. Alexander & Easterbrooks are the gentlemanly proprietors; a country tavern kept by Michael Hahn; a large boarding house of which W

J. Mowry is proprietor; a splendid butcher's shop, owned by Wm. Updike; a livery stable, by Crum; a blacksmith shop; carriage shop; two grocery and provision stores; one tailor's shop; a dress maker and milliner; a harness shop; a boot and shoe store; and eight resident carpenters and joiners.

The railroad companies make this their general wood depot. They also have machine shops; a T rail repairing shop, with steam power, etc. To carry on their branch of industry, for officers, agents, mechanics, and common laborers, it requires about a hundred men, and as about forty trains every twenty-four hours pass through this place, it requires four extensive wells to fill the tanks of the tenders. The shipments and transhipments upon the Chicago, Burlington & Quincy Railroad at this place, amount to about a thousand tons per month; of the Galena & Chicago Union Railroad to about fifteen hundred tons per month, and the Chicago, Iowa & Nebraska Railroad rather less.

As literary and professional men, we have Rev. R. A. Watkins, Rev. S. W. Champlain, J. McConnell, M. D., and Dr. Hall.

The best public school house in DU PAGE County was built in this village the present summer. In the summer of 1856 was organized the "First Congregational Church of Turner," and the following named officers elected: Deacons, Dr. J. McConnell and W. R. Currier; Clerk, J. L. Hagadone. A few days after, a body corporate, with power to hold real estate, was formed under the title of "The Congregational Church and Society of Turner, Illinois," and the following board of trustees was elected, viz.:

Deacon J. McConnell, Deacon W. R. Currier and
Milo Hawks, Esq. The Hon. J. B. Turner, in honor
of whom the village was named, being present,
donated to the society a splendid lot for a meeting
house, and immediate steps were taken to prepare
the way for erecting a house of worship upon it. The
Rev. S. W. Champlain who is now preaching here,
is the first minister employed by the society. There
is an interesting Sabbath school in successful operation here, of some fifty pupils, and an intelligent bible
class numbering over twenty. The library contains
about two hundred volumes."

Winfield is a well cultivated farming town. The
aggregate value of real estate in 1856, was $160,329,
and of personal property $68,007. The town is
divided into eight school districts, all of which are
provided with good school houses. The school section was sold in 1840, at ten shillings per acre, and
the fund thus derived has been increased to $1,282.
The amount paid to teachers in 1857 was $1,126,
and for building and repairing $1,785. The whole
number of scholars in attendance during 1857, was
three hundred and seventy-five.

A company called The Winfield Cavalry, was organized here in 1855. It has now about forty members. G. N. Roundy, captain; and F. G. Kimball,
first lieutenant.

The first town meeting was held at the house of
Charles Gary, in April, 1850. The following are the
names of town officers who have been elected since
that time:

SUPERVISORS:

1850 — William C. Todd.
1851 — William C. Todd.
1852 — William C. Todd.
1853 — Charles Gary.

1854 — Charles Gary.
1855 — Gurdon Roundy,
1856 — Truman W. Smith.
1857 — Charles Gary.

TOWN CLERKS:

1850 — C. L. Shepherd.
1851 — C. L. Shepherd.
1852 — L. Reed Warren.
1853 — B. L. Harlow.

1854 — B. L. Harlow.
1855 — B. L. Harlow.
1856 — B. L. Harlow.
1857 — B. L. Harlow.

OVERSEERS OF THE POOR:

1850 — Charles Gary.
1851 — Charles Gary.
1852 — A. E. Carpenter.
1853 — A. E. Carpenter.

1854 — William C. Todd.
1855 — James Brown.
1856 — T. W. Smith.
1857 — Charles Gary.

COMMISSIONERS OF HIGHWAYS:

1850 — James Brown,
    J. A. Smith,
    Israel Mather.
1851 — James Brown,
    J. A. Smith,
    Israel Mather.
1852 — James Brown,
    J. A. Smith,
    Israel Mather.
1853 — M. M. Kemp,
    John Fairbank,
    G. N. Roundy.

1854 — M. M. Kemp,
    John Fairbank,
    Luther Chandler.
1855 — Ira Woodman,
    Luther. Chandler,
    W. G. Seargent.
1856 — Walter Germain,
    E. Manville,
    W. G. Seargent.
1857 — Walter Germain,
    Charles Bradley,
    H. L. Brown.

CONSTABLES:

1850 — A. C. Graves,
    Thomas M. Griswold.
1851 — A. C. Graves,
    S. B. Kimball.

1852 — A. C. Graves,
    S. B. Kimball.
1853 — A. C. Graves,
    S. B. Kimball.

CONSTABLES — CONTINUED:

1854 — A. C. Graves,   1856 — S. B. Kimball,
         S. B. Kimball.   T. W. Smith.
1855 — S. B. Kimball,   1857 — Reuben Austin.
         T. W. Smith.

COLLECTORS:

1850 — Harvey Higby.   1854 — S. B. Kimball.
1851 — A. C. Graves.   1855 — S. B. Kimball.
1852 — A. C. Graves.   1856 — James Fairbank.
1853 — S. B. Kimball.   1857 — B. L. Harlow.

ASSESSORS:

1850 — Harvy Higby.   1854 — G. N. Roundy.
1851 — A. C. Graves.   1855 —
1852 — Joseph Hudson.   1856 — Daniel Wilson.
1853 — Joseph Hudson.   1857 — James Fairbank.

JUSTICES OF THE PEACE:

1853 — Walter Germain.   1856 — Charles Gary.
1854 — Charles Gary,   B. L. Harlow.
         B. L. Harlow.   1857 — Charles Gary.
1855 — Charles Gary.   B. L. Harlow.
         B. L. Harlow.

HISTORY OF THE TOWN OF WAYNE.

THIS town is in the northwest part of the county. It was first settled in May, 1834. The first family here was that of John Laughlin. Several families settled in different parts of the town during 1834 and the following year. Among these were Capt. W. Hammond, R. Benjamin, Ezra Gilbert, J. V. King, W. Farnsworth, James Davis, Mr. Guild, Joseph McMillen, Isaac Nash, Daniel Dunham, and Ira Albro. The first post-office in the town was at McMillen's Grove. Here, also, the first dwelling and the first school-house were erected. There were but few settlers in the town at the time when the first building was put up, and the owners of it anticipated some trouble in procuring help at the raising. They however, obviated all difficulty on that score by sending for a barrel of whiskey, which, with the subordinate services of only three men, performed the work in an expeditious and satisfactory manner.

No incidents occurred in the early settlement of this town but such as are common to the settlement of all new countries. But little more grain was raised during the first two years than enough to satisfy the demand at home. Prices were extremely low for all kinds of produce, and market was a great way off. The proceeds of a load of corn taken to Chicago were hardly sufficient to defray the expenses of the trip. One of the first settlers informs us, however, that he

S

did realize *three dollars and twelve and a half cents* from the sale of *one load* of forty bushels, which he took to Chicago in 1836, after using twenty-five cents for necessary expenses. There were no difficulties respecting claims in this town, and every claimant received his full quantity of land at the time of the land sale.

The surface of the town is generally uneven, consisting of rolling prairie. Wheat, oats, and corn are the chief agricultural staples. Probably no town in the county is better adapted to the culture of grain.

Fruit is cultivated to a considerable extent in this town, especially the more hardy kinds. Apple trees grow well; but the fruit is rendered an uncertain crop on account of the severity of our winters. Frequent attempts have been made to raise pears, peaches, plums and cherries, without much success. The red English cherry, being the most hardy, does better than any of its class. Mr. Luther Bartlett, of this town, has been more persevering in his efforts to introduce choice kinds of fruit than any other person in this part of the county. · Some four years since he procured, at great expense, from eastern nurseries and by importation from Europe, about five hundred dwarf pear trees, and set them out on his farm. The first two years the trees did well, and gave promise of coming fruitfulness; but during the summer of 1856, which followed an unusually hard winter, for this latitude, they began to exhibit signs of decay. The cold weather of the past winter was also unfavorable, and gave an impetus to the work of destruction commenced by the former season, which has almost desolated the field. There are now scarcely a dozen trees living of the five hundred planted four years ago. We think the experiment of Mr. Bartlett fully determines that this region is not adapted to the raising of choice kinds of fruit.

This town is not well supplied with wood and timber from its own resources. The "Little Woods," just over the line in Kane County, are chiefly owned by the inhabitants of this town, and afford convenient supplies of both fuel and timber. Good water is abundant. The west branch of the Du Page runs through the east part of the town. Streams of less note and many living springs of pure water are found in all parts of the town.

The attention of the farmers has been of late directed to the introduction of "blooded" stock. Wool is becoming an important article among agriculturalists. Several large flocks of fine wool sheep are owned here, among which is that of Luther Bartlett, which has numbered over 1,000. The farms throughout the town present unmistakable evidence of thrift and industry; the dwellings display neatness and taste; and the barns are constructed on a scale commensurate with the great and growing demands of the harvest fields. Mr. Daniel Dunham, of this town, erected a barn in 1856, the dimensions of which are fifty by one hundred feet. It has sufficient capacity for 100 head of cattle and 300 tons of hay. It cost about $4,000, and is probably the largest and best arranged barn in northern Illinois. Land in this town is worth from $30 to $40 per acre. The farms range from two to five hundred acres. Among the best farms in the

north part of the town are those of Messrs. L. Bartlett,
W. Hammond, and L. Pierce; and in the south, those
of Messrs. D. Dunham and Ira Albro.

There are seven school districts in the town, in all
of which schools are sustained. The whole number of
scholars who attended the different schools during the
winter of 1857, was 218. The school section was
mostly occupied by settlers before it came into market,
and by an agreement among the pioneers of the town,
that all who chanced to settle upon it should obtain
their lands at government price, it was sold at ten
shillings per acre. The school fund thus obtained has
increased to about $1,300.

The Congregational Church is the only organized
religious body in this town. This society was formed
in 1842, or thereabouts, and worshipped in the school
house at the centre, until 1849, when it united with
the school district in erecting a building suitable for a
church and school-house. From some dissatisfaction
arising from joint occupancy or ownership, the society
soon after bought out the interest of the district, and
became vested with the sole ownership. By the aid of
the Home Missionary Society, the pulpit has been
regularly supplied by a settled minister. The Rev.
Mr. Foot was the first pastor. After his dismissal,
the Rev. Mr. Parker became pastor; and he was succeeded by the Rev. Mr. Sykes, the present pastor, who
has served the society acceptably for several years.
The Sabbath school connected with this church has
between forty and fifty scholars. Several other denominations hold meetings in different parts of the town.

The first settlement at the Centre, *alias*, "Gimletville," *alias*, Orangeville, was made in 1836, by Mr. Guild. Mr. A. Guild is the post-master at this place. It is a small settlement, containing one church, one store, and a few dwelling houses. There is a small settlement at the railroad station, consisting of two stores, one hotel, a post-office, station house, and several dwellings. The station is thirty-three miles west of Chicago. S. Dunham was the first settler at this place.

There are no manufacturing establishments in the town, if we exclude the manufacture of brooms, which has been carried on pretty extensively at Wayne Centre. The present population is about 1,100. The town is peaceable and healthful, being cursed by neither lawyers nor doctors.

We give below a list of town officers, who have been elected since the town of Wayne was organized:

SUPERVISORS:

1850 — Luther Pierce.	1854 — Luther Bartlett.
1851 — "	1855 — Luther Pierce.
1852 — "	1856 — Ira Albro.
1853 — Luther Bartlett.	1857 — Charles Adams.

TOWN CLERKS:

1850 — Ira Albro.	1854 — S. W. Moffatt.
1851 — Charles Smith.	1855 — "
1852 — "	1856 — J. Q. Adams.
1853 — "	1857 — "

OVERSEERS OF POOR:

1850 — Charles Smith.	1854 — Ira Green.
1851 — H. Sherman.	1855 — W. K. Guild.
1852 — Ira Green.	1856 — Joel Wiant.
1853 — Samuel Adams.	1857 — Charles Adams.

ASSESSORS :

1850 — S. W. Moffatt.
1851 — Charles Adams.
1852 —   "
1853 —   "

1854 — J. Clisbee.
1855 — C. Adams.
1856 — John Glos.
1857 — Charles Smith.

COMMISSIONERS OF HIGHWAYS :

1850 — Charles Adams, Myron Smith, Henry Sherman.
1851 — Joel Wiant, S. W. Moffatt, L. Bartlett.
1852 — D. Sterns, J. Clisbee, J. Wiant.
1853 — J. Clisbee, D. L. Whelock, D. Dunham.

1854 — A. D. Moffatt, Ira Green, D. Dunham.
1855 — S. Adams, G. Reed, H. V. Sayer.
1856 — H. V. Sayer, A. Fairbank, J. O. Haviland.
1857 — W. H. Moffatt, W. K. Guild, S. Adams.

JUSTICES OF THE PEACE :

1850 — E. L. Guild, S. McNitt.
1851 — E. L. Guild, John Glos.
1852 —   "   "
1853 — L. F. Sanderson, John Glos.

1854 — Charles Smith, John Glos.
1855 —   "   "
1856 —   "   "
1857 — Samuel Adams, Charles Smith.

CONSTABLES :

1850 — D. C. Nash.
1851 — H. Ford.
1852 —   "
1853 —   "

1854 — S. Adams.
1855 — E. C. Guild.
1856 — Geo. Rinehart.
1857 —   "

COLLECTORS :

1850 — D. C. Nash.
1851 — H. Ford.
1852 —   "
1853 — Ira Green.

1854 — S. Adams.
1855 — Geo. Rinehart.
1856 — M. J. Hammond.
1857 — Lyman Flower.

HISTORY OF THE TOWN OF DOWNER'S GROVE.

The following sketch, as far as quoted, has been kindly furnished us by the Hon. Walter Blanchard.

"This town is in the southeast corner of Du Page County, and embraces nearly one and one third townships of land. It was first settled in 1832, by Pierce Downer (not by Wells and Grant, as stated in our table) who emigrated to Illinois from Jefferson county, New York.

"He was at that time a man of unusual physical powers, energetic, and capable of great endurance. He is still living at the advanced age of seventy-five years, and although his bodily health is somewhat impaired, more by the weight of years than by disease, yet his mind retains the full vigor of youth. His habits are temperate, industrious and studious. In order to impart a correct understanding of the early settlement of this part of the county, it may be as well to state that Downer's grove, proper, is a body of timber, containing about one section, and lies mostly on sections six and seven of township 38. N. of R. 11. E. It derived its name from the first settler who made his claim in and near it. Subsequently the whole township received the same name. Mr. Downer's settlement was followed the next year by his son Stephen, Mr. Wells and Mr. Cooley. The claim made by Mr. Downer was on the north side of the grove; that of his son was on the east side; and that of Messrs. Wells and Cooley was at the southeast extremity of the large prairie which stretches away some three miles toward the north, five miles toward the south, and three miles toward the west. An important object of the first settlers was to secure a large amount of good timber, hence we find most of our pioneers made their claims on the borders of the groves and forests.

"The country about the grove had not then been surveyed, and the settlers marked their claims in divers ways; some by sticking stakes; some by plowing a furrow around them; while others, more greedy, were like Franklin's philosopher, anxious to grasp more than they could hold, and claimed all the eye could survey, at one long look, in each direction. From this inordinate development of acquisitiveness, many quarrels originated respecting claims. With all the broad extent of unoccupied territory around them, it would seem impossible that men, in order to protect their rights, should have been obliged to make a display of squatter sovereignty; but so it was. The first trouble about claims in this town was between Mr. Downer and Messrs. Cooley and Wells, and here is Mr. Downer's version of the matter.

"'I went to Chicago one day to buy some provisions, and on returning, thought I saw some one working near the northeast corner of the grove. I went home and deposited my cargo (a back load), and although very tired, went out to reconnoitre my premises. To my great surprise I found Wells and Cooley had commenced erecting a cabin on my claim. I went to a thicket close by and cut a hickory gad, but found I had no power to use it, for I was so mad that it took my strength all away. So I sat down and tried to cool off a little, but my excitement only *cooled* from a sort of violent passion to deep and downright indignation. To think that my claim should be invaded, and that too, by the only two white men besides myself then at the grove, made the vessel of my wrath to simmer like a pent sea over a burning volcano. I could sit still no longer. So I got up and advanced towards them, and the nearer I approached the higher rose the temperature of my anger, which, by the time I got to them, was flush up to the boiling point. I said nothing, but pitched into them, *shelalah* in hand, and for about five minutes did pretty good execution. But becoming exhausted and being no longer able to keep them at bay, they grappled with me, threw me on the ground, and after holding me down a short time, they seemed to come to the conclusion that 'discretion was the better part of valor' and let me up, when they ran one way and I the other, no doubt leaving blood enough upon the field of action to induce a stray prairie wolf to stop and take a passing snuff as he went that way. But, sir, they did'nt come again to jump my claim.'

"The Grove at an early day was one of the favorite camping grounds of an Indian chief of the Potawattomies, called Waubansie. Here he used to come with his warriors and remain for several days together, and always continued on the most friendly terms with the settlers.

"The first impression of emigrants to this region was

*8

that it could never be generally settled on account of
the scarcity of timber, and up to 1836, only eight or
ten families had settled at the grove. In 1835, Mr.
I. P. Blodgett one of the first settlers at the east
branch in Lisle, sold out his claim there, and bought
that of *Jumper* Wells in this town.

"Mr. Blodgett was a blacksmith by trade, a most
worthy man and really a great accession to the settlement, not only as a mechanic, but as a correct and
upright man. He was formerly from Massachusetts,
and possessed New England habits of industry, morals
and economy, which did much for the improvement
of society in the new settlement. Here Mr. Blodgett
built a shop, and, at that time, made the best plows
to be found in the country. We would not be understood to mean by this remark that they were better
than the modern productions of Messrs. Vaughan and
Peck, but those who know the difficulties which were
encountered before the *scouring* plows were introduced, can properly appreciate the good qualities of
the plows made by Mr. Blodgett. It is true that the
operation was something like plowing with a hemlock
limb, yet they were the best plows we had, and so we
used them. To one who has never held a plow that
would not *scour*, all this may be uninteresting, but
ask an old settler, What would be the severest test of
human endurance? and he will no doubt answer,
'Being obliged to use a plow that will not clear
itself.' If a man can do that guiltless of profanity
he is unquestionably an upright person.

"Of the second class of settlers who came in between
1836 and 1839, may be named, Asa Carpenter, Dexter

Stanley, Levi C. Aldrich, Garry Smith, Samuel Curtis, J. R. Adams, David Page, Henry Carpenter, Walter Blanchard, J. W. Walker and Horace Aldrich. The county at this time was being settled very fast by new comers, and the interests of the settlers began to clash. The claims extended around the entire grove. No questions arose respecting prairie claims, for it was the timber that all were after. Mr. Horace Aldrich had come in from Jefferson county, New York, and Mr. Downer had selected a claim of timber and prairie for him. It was not long before he discovered that Asa Carpenter was intruding (we dare not say trespassing) upon his timber claim. Mr. Carpenter was cutting timber for fencing, and swore he would persist in doing so, for he had as good a right there as any other man. The neighbors advised with him, but it was of no use. They remonstrated, but the effect was the same. They finally threatened, but this only made the old man swear like the army in Flanders. The neighbors then held a consultation among themselves, and decided to apply squatter sovereignty to the old man's case. Accordingly they met at a stated time, and went to the place where they found him busily engaged getting out rails. They requested him to leave the claim, but the old man swore positively that he would do no such thing. One of the settlers proceeded to cut a long hickory gad, and the powerful hand that had wielded the same persuasive argument on a former occasion, was again called into requisition. After about a dozen blows had been industriously applied to his back and legs, Carpenter proposed a brief cessation of hostilities, that he might argue the question with them. The request was complied with, but the conversation soon waxed warm, and the hickory was again applied with redoubled vigor. This was too much for poor human nature to bear, and Carpenter, putting every power of pedestrianism which he had, in operation, left the crowd without even thanking them for this first practical lesson in squatter sovreignty.

"This effectually settled the claim difficulty, although some legal proceedings grew out of the affair.

"These were the only instances where personal violence was employed to settle claim feuds. Claim protecting societies were formed similar to those already noticed in another part of this book; agreements were entered into to deed and re-deed, and when the lands were surveyed and came into market, each settler received all he had justly claimed.

"The first school in this town was started in 1839, and taught by Norman G. Hurd. It was kept in the back part of a log house, owned by Mr. Samuel Curtis. This was a private enterprise, and by shifting from one old building to another, the school was kept going from five to six months during the year, for some four years.

"In 1844 a school-house was built, and is yet occupied by the district. For a full description of this building we refer the reader to a report of Rev. Hope Brown, while commissioner, by which its reputation suffered some, but since the Reverend gentleman has left the county, the old house stands fair.

"What has been said relates more particularly to the settlement of Downer's grove proper, than to the township of that name, for the reason that all, excepting five or six sections of the township, was upon the old Indian survey, and not subject to the difficulties which attended the settlement of the unsurveyed portion of it.

"It may be said, and truthfully, that, in a moral and physical point of view, the inhabitants of this township stand on high vantage ground; and yet they claim to be no better, and no smarter than their neighbors. In concluding our chapter on this town, we propose to sketch some of the incidents and practices, more common at an early day than now.

"Until within a few years, this part of the county was infested with wolves, which were a source of great annoyance to the whole community. The farmers, however, were the principal sufferers by their depredations; for sometimes whole flocks were destroyed and scattered by them in a single night. To rid the country of these mischievous animals, it was the custom for all who were able to "bear arms," to rally once every year for a wolf hunt, which was usually a scene of much amusement, and oftentimes of the most intense excitement. These expeditions were conducted in various ways. The general hunt, which was perhaps the most common, was conducted upon the following plan:

"Notice of the time of starting, the extent of country to be traveled over, and of the place of meeting, which was usually at the common centre of the circle of territory to be traversed, was first given to all the participants in the hunt. At an early hour on the morning of the day appointed, the hunters assembled and chose a captain for each company, whose duty it was to station members of the company at short intervals

upon the circumference of the circle alluded to, and
then the game was completely surrounded. At a given
time the line of hunters began their march, and when
they had approached near enough to the centre to close
in and form a solid line, they halted and remained sta-
tionary, while the captains advanced with their sharp
shooters to ascertain whether any game had been surrounded. If an unlucky wolf or deer had been drawn
into the snare, upon making his appearance before the
lines, he was sure to be riddled by rifle balls. We
have been informed by one who frequently participated
in hunts of this kind, that he had known of sixty
wolves and as many deer being killed in one day. This
mode of hunting the deer seemed altogether too cruel
and cowardly in the eyes of some, but no scruples
were entertained in thus exterminating the mischievous, thieving wolves. To see the harmless deer penned
up with no chance of escaping, darting about bewildered, with eyes almost starting from their sockets, and
then to see them slaughtered in the manner described,
appeared cruel in the extreme. The mode of hunting
wolves adopted by the settlers at Downer's grove, was
different from that described, and obviated the appearance of cruelty in slaying the deer.

"The wolf hunt was a source of amusement in this
town for years, and whenever a wolf dared to show
his head above the prairie grass, the boys were instantly in pursuit of him. The pursuers usually went
on horseback, carrying in the hand a short club, and
the captain of the company was the one who had the
swiftest horse. The plan of action was to spread out
in every direction and scour the prairie until the game

was started, when by a peculiar yell, the whole company was called together and the chase commenced. Every horse was now put to his utmost speed, and with his rider, would go flying over the prairie like the wind. It is utterly impossible to describe the wild excitement that attended the wolf chase. Generally a race of from three to five miles would bring *Mr. Wolf* down; then, the day's sport would be ended, and the party would return home in a sort of triumphal procession, bearing the fallen hero. Such reckless, headlong riding was attended with much hazard, and although no serious accident ever happened to the riders, yet it is surmised that the horses might have suffered from ring-bones and spavins induced by undue speed.

"At one of the last of these hunts a circumstance occurred which may be classed with the serio-comic, as it at first assumed a serious phase, and then, as circumstances changed, became thoroughly ludicrous. On a cold, blustering morning in January, 1846, the *boys* (men) started out for a hunt. Wolves were becoming scarce, and the party wandered off some five or six miles, to the north of what was then known as the Duzenberry claim. The new settlers had commenced fencing their lands, and at several places before coming to this claim the party had been obliged to dismount and remove the obstruction, but here they found a *ditch* fence, which terminated at a great distance on the open prairie, and was built upon the supposition that the cattle could not, or would not go around it, consequently there was no fence on the back side.

"The snow had drifted very deep on the side of this

fence opposite to the party, and although their horses had been trained to jumping, yet an attempt to leap it would only land both horse and rider floundering in a deep snow bank.

"While holding a consultation to decide upon some method of surmounting the barrier, a wolf started from a thicket and crossed the path only a few rods from them. Every man instantly wheeled into line, and as quick as thought darted on after the affrighted animal. In the language of one of the company, 'the wolf was a large, gaunt old chap, and promised to give us a long pull and a strong pull.' Gard had a fine smart little pony, that would run like the wind, and he led the company. The chase led us far out into the prairie, and before long we found ourselves running inside of the fences on the Duzenberry claim, in a southerly direction, and would soon have to clear one of the ditch fences. There were fifteen horsemen spread out in a line, every man plying the whip and spur, and every horse at the top of his speed. We came to the fence, which the wolf cleared about two rods in advance of Gard, and as he came up, his horse seeming to partake of the general excitement, made a bold leap, clearing the ditch fence in fine style; but unfortunately landing in a snow bank, the horse stumbled and fell, plunging entirely out of sight — at the same time throwing Gard over his head and burying him beneath the snow. To the party in the rear it appeared as though the earth had swallowed up both horse and rider, as the fence and snow partially concealed the scene from their view. Not a rider attempted to check the headlong speed of his horse until he had cleared the fence. Some of the foremost horses made a second leap, which carried them completely over the prostrate horse of the first rider. The first thought was for Gard. The general exclamation was, 'He is dead!' and an awful gloom sat upon the countenance of all. While thus solemnly ruminating upon his almost inevitable fate, the party were not a little astounded at beholding him rise, Phœnix like, from his bed of snow, among the floundering horses.

Among the company was Alden Stanley, a noble, fine fellow, (alas! he has gone to his long home,) who was standing by, very much excited. He wore a buffalo coat, made like a frock, cut off at the knees. Soon after Gard came out of the snow, his horse, for the first time, suddenly made his appearance, and seemed very much frightened. The first thing that attracted his attention was Stanley's buffalo coat, and wheeling, he kicked at it like a flash of lightning, carrying away one entire skirt. At this juncture the wolf was discovered about a mile distant, standing upon an elevation and looking back over his shoulder. Taking it all in all, this was one of the most laughable farces I ever witnessed, passing, as it did, from one extreme of feeling to another, and so suddenly too, that none knew whether to laugh or cry until we were just ready to remount and resume the chase, when it was first discovered by Stanley that he had lost one of his coat skirts. The attention of the company was drawn to the fact by Stanley's remarking that some of his comrades had dressed their sheep skin; and this brought down the house with a loud roar. After mounting their horses, the company started again,

jehu-like, in pursuit of the wolf; and within five
minutes from the time of the new start *Mr. Wolf* had
surrendered unconditionally to superior force. I think
the wolves even, were superstitious about the Downer's
Grove boys, and made it a practice to give up at once
when *they* were on their track. Many of the *boys* are
still living, and reside at or near the grove. Of these
may be mentioned Hon. W. Blanchard, D. C. Stanley,
John Stanley, L. Stanley, Emerson Stanley, Charles
Curtis, E. E. Downer. Ah, when we come to call
the roll, there are more missing than we thought for.
And now where are they? Well, the Adamses are in
California, the Curtises are at Wheaton, Henry Blodgett is an attorney at Waukegan, Israel Blodgett is in
California, Daniel has gone to his last resting place,
Asel is in railroad business, and — and — in fact, there
are not as many left as I thought there were; but there
are yet enough to get up a good game of ball now and
then."

There are four societies of Protestants and one of
Catholics in the town. The Methodist Episcopal society was the first to establish preaching at the Grove,
which was as early as 1839. Father Ged, as he was
called — an itinerant preacher of that denomination —
used to come across the prairies on foot from Barber's
Corners, with undeviating regularity, to preach to the
people here. The adverse changes of the weather
made no difference with him; and wherever he had
an appointment he was sure to meet it, in spite of heat
or cold, wind or rain. Nothing but a sincere desire
to do good could have induced him to undergo, volun-
tarily, the hardships to which his itinerancy subjected

him. He succeeded in forming a small society at the Grove, where preaching has been regularly sustained; and the infant church has grown to be quite numerous. This society has a good meeting house, which was built in 1852. We give some statistics relating to this church. The society was regularly organized in June, 1851, by Rev. Mr. Grundy, with the following named members: J. P. Cotes, Mary C. Cotes, Nancy E. Cotes, Norman G. Hurd, Antoinette Hurd, Eliza Bakeman, Anne Page, Lester Hunt, and Dorcas Hunt.

PASTORS:

Rev. Stephen R. Beggs, served one year.
Rev. S. Stover, served two years.
Rev. H. S. Trumbull, served two years.
Rev. S. Washburn, present pastor.

The whole number of members on record is thirty-six. The number of Sabbath school scholars is eighty-five; and the number of volumes in the library is three hundred.

The Methodists have another society and church in that division of the south part of this township called Cass. The first effort towards organizing the church at Cass, was made by the Rev. Elihu Springer, in 1834.

The following are the names of the subsequent pastors, as near as ascertained:

Rev. Mr. Blackwell,	Rev. Mr. Jenks,
" " Wilder,	" S. Stover,
" " Martin,	" L. R. Ellis,
" John Nason,	" J. R. Wood,
" O. A. Walker,	" George Reack,
" Nathan Jewett,	" W. A. Chambers,
" J. M. Hinman,	" John Grundy,

Rev. M. Hanna,   Rev. H. S. Trumbull,
"   S. Stover,   "   S. Washburn, present pastor.
"   Mr. Wilcox,   "   J W. Agard, Presiding Elder.

The original members of this church were Hart L.
Cobb, Betsey Cobb, George Jackson, Louisa Hill, and
John Covely. There are now twenty members of the
society, forty members of the Sabbath school, and
three hundred volumes in the library.

A society of Congregationalists was organized in
this town in March, 1837, by the Rev. N. C. Clark.
The first members were G. E. Parmalee, John A.
Richards, Dexter Stanley, Henry Puffer, Nancy Stanley, Susan S. Parmalee, Lucia Puffer, Elizabeth M.
Puffer, and Hannah P. Puffer. The pastors in regular succession, have been :

Rev. Orange Lyman,   Rev. Alanson Alvord,
"   Romulus Barnes,   "   Francis Leonard.
                    Rev. George Langdon.

The number of members, and other information respecting this church, we have been unable to obtain.

The Baptist Church was organized under the labors
of the Rev. Mr. Holt, in 1853, with about thirty members. Among the most active members in forming
this society were Edward Goodenough, Albin Lull, and
Norman Gilbert. The same year it was organized,
the society erected a church edifice, which was an
honor to those who projected and carried out the enterprise. No further particulars respecting this church
have been obtained.

The Catholics have a church and society at Cass,
called the church of St. Patrick. A house of worship
was erected in February, 1846, and the society at that

time numbered thirty-four. The following table will show who have been its pastors, and also the number of members at different periods since its organization :

1846 — Rev.	John Ingoldsby,	Pastor.	— No. of members,			34
1848 —	" Dennis Ryan,	"	" " "			37
1851 —	" Michael O'Donnell,	"	" " "			40
1853 —	" James Fitzgerald,	"	" " "			39
1854 —	" James McGowan,	"	" " "			41
Feb. 1856 —	" John McGloflen,	"	" " "			44
Nov. 1856 —	" Michael Harley,	"	" " "			47
1857 —	" Nicholas Mulvey,	present pastor.				

The population of Downer's Grove at this time is about 1,200. The people are chiefly engaged in agricultural pursuits, and hence the town contains no villages of much importance. Near the north east part of the town there is quite a smart little "huddle," generally known as Brush Hill; but at present we believe it is dignified by the title of Fullersburg. The first settlement at Fullersburg was made by Orente Grant, in 1836.

There is another settlement at Lower Cass, in the south part of the town, on the Chicago and Joliet road. The first settlers here were Albin Lull, Dr. Bronson, Hart L. Cobb, Thomas Andrus, and H. Martin. Of this settlement it may be said that its inhabitants are an industrious, enterprising, "good set of folks," — a high compliment to pay to any community.

The original fund derived from the sale of the school lands was $800. It has been increased by interest, and is now $1,063 72.

The amount paid to teachers in 1856 was $1,048 98. The number of school districts in the town is nine. The highest rate of compensation paid to teachers is

$25 per month. The average number who attend school is about 500; and the average number of months in the year, in which schools are taught, is eight. The average monthly compensation of female teachers has been about fourteen dollars.

Names of town officers for the town of Downer's Grove since its organization, in 1850:

SUPERVISORS:

1850 — L. K. Hatch,	1854 — G. W. Alderman.
1851 — Walter Blanchard,	1855 — Walter Blanchard.
1852 — "	1856 — S. F. Daniels.
1853 — "	1857 — S. DeGolyer.

TOWN CLERKS:

1850 — A. Havens.	1854 — A. Havens.
1851 — "	1855 — C. H. Carpenter.
1852 — "	1856 — G. S. Rogers.
1853 — "	1857 — W. H. Dixon.

ASSESSORS:

1850 — O. B. Herrick.	1854 — Lyman Clifford.
1851 — George Barber.	1855 — "
1852 — "	1856 — "
1853 — "	1857 — A. H. Blodgett.

COLLECTORS:

1850 — Peter Warden.	1854 — M. Walton.
1851 — G. Paige.	1855 — E. H. Gleason.
1852 — H. L. Cobb.	1856 — "
1853 — E. H. Gleason.	1857 — George Wheeler.

OVERSEERS OF POOR:

1850 — Albin Lull.	1854 — Daniel Roberts.
1851 — "	1855 — "
1852 — J. Blodgett.	1856 — John Oldfield.
1853 — "	1857 — "

COMMISSIONERS OF HIGHWAYS:

1850 — Silas Culver, W. Lutiens, L. M. Lull.

1851 — John Marvin, A. H. Blodgett, G. Gilbert.

1852 — E. Thatcher, K. Martin, H. Andrews.

1853 — A. Lull, E. Thatcher, G. Paige.

1854 — J. Craigmile, H. Lyon, B. Fuller.

1855 — J. Craigmile, M. Duello, M Sucher.

1856 — A. G. Cobb, H. Lyman, M. Sucher.

1857 — W. H. Clark, J. Oldfield, G. Prescott.

JUSTICES OF THE PEACE:

1850 — John Marsell, Benjamin Fuller.

1851 — S. F. Daniels.

1857 — M. B. Tirtlot, S. J. Ackley.

CONSTABLES:

1850 — Peter Warden, Joseph Boyd.

1851 — Milton Barr, Peter Braman.

1853 — S. W. Franklin.

1854 — S. W. Franklin, Luther Couch.

1855 — E Gleason.

1856 — T. O. Roberts

HISTORY OF THE TOWN OF YORK.

WE are unable to give as complete a history of this
town as we could desire, although we have tried faithfully to obtain the necessary information to do so.
We cannot but believe that there are many incidents
connected with its early settlement that would, to say
the least, be of interest to the inhabitants of the township, if not to the general reader, notwithstanding
the contrary opinion, which prevails among the early
settlers.

York was first settled in the spring of 1834, by
Elisha Fish. His claim was on the south east quarter
of section thirty-five, where his widow still lives. The
next who came in was Henry Reader, who settled in
1835, on the south west quarter of section thirty-five.
Luther Morton settled soon after on section seven;
Benjamin Fuller on section twenty-five; Nicholas
Torode, sen., on section twenty-seven; and in April,
1836, John Talmadge removed to this town from
Brush Hill, where he had lived since 1834, and settled on the south east quarter of section twenty-three.
In May, 1836, there were several families added to
the settlement. Among these were the families of
Jesse Atwater, Edward Eldridge, and David Tal-
madge. In July of the same year, the settlement was
increased by the families of Jacob W. Fuller and
David Thurston. In 1837, Sheldon Peek, W. Churchill, Zerais Cobb, John Glos and John Bohlander

came in and settled on what is now called the St.
Charles road. John Thrasher came in about the same
time, and settled on section thirty. The first settlers
of this town were preëminently fitted to endure the
trials incident to frontier life. They were "made of
the right sort of stuff," and advanced boldly with the
standard of civilization, regardless of danger, and
knowing no dread of hardships. Many of them had
been brought up on the borders of civilization, and
were thoroughly inured to all the privations of pioneer
life. Perhaps no town in this county can justly claim
to itself a more hardy, daring class of pioneers. John
Talmadge, whose name has already been mentioned
among the early settlers of this town, was for several
years a soldier in the U. S. army. In that capacity
he was in the service of his country during the war
of 1812, and in several battles fought valiantly under
our national banner. Although his head is now
"silvered o'er with age," yet that quenchless spirit of
patriotism which fired his youth still glows within his
breast and flashes from his fading eye.

This township contains thirty-six square miles of
land, and has a soil, cultivation, vales, fields, land-
scapes and scenery, which would not suffer in com-
parison with many sections of country more widely
and favorably known. It affords an agreeable variety
of surface and soil, well adapted to the wants of the
husbandman, and, with proper cultivation, yields him
most bountiful harvests for the support of the multi-
tudes dependent upon his industry.

The principal stream is Salt creek, which runs
through the town from north to south.

9

Most of the first settlers were originally from the State of New York, and when the inhabitants were called upon to give a name to their precinct, that of York was selected with but few dissenting voices.

The manufactures of this town are unimportant. A steam flouring mill is now in operation at Brush Hill, owned by F. Gray. This mill has two run of stones, and is the only manufactory of much importance in the town. The Galena railroad runs through the town, and upon it two young and thriving villages have sprung up, like Minerva from the brain of Jove, full armed and ready for effective service. These are at Cottage Hill and at Babcock's Grove.

"The village of Cottage Hill is pleasantly situated on the line of the Galena and Chicago Union Railroad, sixteen miles west from Chicago. The first settler here was J. L. Hovey, who came from Painesville, Ohio. He built a small house in 1843, which he kept as a hotel, it being favorably known by the farmers of the Fox and Rock river counties, who then teamed their own produce to Chicago, as the 'Hill Cottage.' The 'Hill' proper lies half a mile from the railroad, and commands as fine a prospect of prairie, cultivated farms, groves, cottages, and railroad trains, as one could desire to behold. This place being but 15 1-2 miles from the centre of business in Chicago; having good water, pure air, and railroad trains hourly passing — all of which stop here — must soon become known to those who would find for themselves and families, at a convenient distance from the city, a retreat from the noise and dust of its hot and crowded streets."

The railroad was completed to this place in 1849, since which time the village has been chiefly built up. It now contains one hotel, five stores, several manufacturing establishments, a railroad passenger house, some thirty or forty dwellings, and about 200 inhabitants. A fine edifice is now in process of erection, to be used as a church and school house. There is no other church building in the town, although there are several organized religious societies, which hold their meetings in the school houses in different parts of the town.

Babcock's Grove is a pleasant village, of some 200 inhabitants, situated about five miles west of Cottage Hill, on the Galena road. It is an active, business-like place, and promises to become a town of considerable importance. It has a good hotel, several stores, and a number of fine residences.

The present population of the town of York is not far from 1500. The Germans have settled pretty thickly in some parts of the town, and among them may be found some of the best farmers in the county. They are frugal, industrious, and honest, as a class, and manage their farms with superior agricultural skill.

There are three post offices in the town. George Fuller is post master at York Centre, Jerry Bates at Cottage Hill, and J. B. Hull at Babcock's Grove.

York has the largest school fund of any town in Du Page county. The school section was sold at five dollars per acre, creating an original fund of $3,200. It is now near $3,500. The highest rate of compensation paid to teachers is $25 per month; the lowest is $10 per month. The amount paid for teachers' wages amounts to about $800 annually. There are eight public schools taught in the township, which are attended by 400 scholars. The average number of months in the year in which schools are taught is eight, and the average number of scholars in each school is forty.

We would here remark that the sources from which we have obtained the statistics relating to this town have *not* been the most reliable, and if we find errors have occurred, it will not be to us a matter of very great surprise.

The following is a list of officers for the town of York since its organization in 1850.

SUPERVISORS.

1850 — Edward Eldridge,
    Gerry Bates, appointed to
    fill vacancy.
1851 — Gerry Bates.
1852 — Gerry Bates.
1853 — Webster Burbanks.

1853 — Hiram Whittemore, appointed to fill vacancy.
1854 — Asa Knapp.
1855 — Robert Reed.
1856 — Robert Reed.
1857 — Frederick Gray.

TOWN CLERKS:

1850 — Allen M. Wright,
    Charles Mather, appointed
    to fill vacancy.
1851 — Peter R. Torode.
1852 — Peter R. Torode.

1853 — Adam Glos.
1854 — Adam Glos.
1855 — Adam Glos.
1856 — Adam Glos.
1857 — Adam Glos.

ASSESSORS.

1850 — George Fuller.
1851 — John Talmadge.
1852 — Webster Burbanks,
    P. R. Torode, appointed to
    fill vacancy.

1853 — James A. E. Barras.
1854 — Orrin Newell.
1855 — George Fuller.
1856 — George Fuller.
1857 — George Fuller.

COLLECTORS.

1850 — Adam Glos.
1851 — Adam Glos.
1852 — Benjamin Plummer.
1853 — David Fuller.

1854 — Ansel Bates.
1855 — Lewis Eldridge.
1856 — Lewis Eldridge.
1857 — Lewis Eldridge.

OVERSEERS OF POOR.

1850 — Robert Reed.
1851 — Burgess Austin.
1852 — Burgess Austin.
1853 — Asa Knapp.

1854 — Layton Collar.
1855 — John Thrasher.
1856 — John Thrasher.
1857 — John Thrasher.

COMMISSIONERS OF HIGHWAYS.

1850 — James L. Snow,
 John Thrasher,
 Reuben Mink.
1851 — Asa Knapp,
 John Thrasher.
 Frederick Gray.
1852 — Lewis Wood.
 Samuel Loy.
 Frederick Gray.
1853 — George Fuller,
 Hiram Whittemore,
 Frederick Gray,
 G. H. Atwater, appointed
 to fill vacancy.

1854 — Lewis Wood,
 John B. Bohlander,
 E. A. Hall,
 George Fuller, appointed
 to fill vacancy.
1855 — Lewis Wood,
 John P. Bohlander,
 Warren Kittell.
1856 — Milo Porter,
 John Norbury,
 Warren Kittell.
1857 — William Boyer,
 John Norbury,
 Warren Kittell.

JUSTICES OF THE PEACE.

1850 — David Thurston.
 Orson D. Richards.
1852 — Cyrenus Litchfield, elected
 to fill vacancy.
1854 — Cyrenus Litchfield.
 Moses Gray.

1855 — Thomas Filer, elected to
 fill vacancy.
1856 — John Thrasher, elected to
 fill vacancy.
1857 — Milo Porter, elected to fill
 vacancy.

CONSTABLES.

1850 — David Fuller.
        C. W. Richardson.
1853 — D. Mono, elected to fill vacancy.
1854 — John Norbury, elected to fill vacancy.

1855 — John Norbury,
        John G. Kleinschrot.
1856 — Lewis Eldridge, elected to fill vacancy.

SUMMARY.

Du Page County was first settled by the whites in 1830. It was surveyed in 18 —; was separated from Cook county, of which it previously formed a part, and became a distinct organization by act of legislature, approved February 9th, 1839. By the census of 1850, its population was 12,807; and assuming a uniform ratio of increase drawn from the census of preceding years, it is now nearly 15,000. It has 3,000 dwellings; 2,850 families; 10 villages; 7 different religious denominations; 22 churches; 3,150 communicants; 2,250 children and youth who attend Sabbath school. The following is a list of the post offices in the county:

PLACE.	NAME OF P. M.
Naperville	Robert Naper,
Big Woods, (Naperville)	John Warne,
Addison	Henry Bartling,
Sagone	S. D. Pierce,
York Center	George Fuller,
Cottage Hill (York)	Gerry Bates.
Babcock's Grove (York)	J. B. Hull,
Bonaparte	H. Dodge,
Downer's Grove	
Warrenville (Winfield)	Col. J. M. Warren,
Winfield, "	Andrew Van Deusen,
Turner, "	

PLACE.	NAME OF P. M.
Wheaton (Milton)........................	C. K. W. Howard,
Danby, "	David Kelly,
Wayne.................................	S. Dunham,
Wayne Center.........................	Albert Guild,
Lisle................................	John Thompson,
Brush Hill	B. Fuller,
Cass (Downer's Grove).................	G. W. Alderman,
Bloomingdale	Hiram Cody,

There are eighteen miles of railroad in this county, upon which seven enterprising villages are situated. We give a statement of freight handled at the several stations, in pounds, and also the amount of cash receipts for freight.

STATIONS.	FREIGHT.	RECEIPTS.
Cottage Hill.........................	4,275,680	$3,605 23
Babcock's Grove	2,107,700	1,404 63
Danby................................	2,234,660	2,728 02
Wheaton	7,544,220	5,880 26
Winfield.............................	4,671,820	3,036 25
Junction	5,480,820	7,164 47
Wayne	1,900,760	1,633 81

The statement in another part of the book, that Winfield forwards the greatest amount of freight is incorrect, as it appears by the last report of the G. & C. U. Railroad Company, that less tonnage goes from that station, than from Cottage Hill or Junction.

With the above brief summary our history is ended. Enough has been said to give, as we believe, a pretty correct view of the past and present condition of Du PAGE County. If by this compilation anything is rescued from oblivion that will be of consequence

to our future historian, the authors are satisfied; and
if the work is received with satisfaction among those
early settlers, within whose early recollection all the
incidents herein detailed have transpired, they will
feel doubly rewarded for their labors.

While writing these concluding remarks, news has
reached us of the death of Eli Northam, at the advanced age of eighty-seven years. He was an early
settler in the south part of this county, and among
the foremost in establishing and sustaining our first
Christian church. It is fitting to insert here the following brief tribute to his memory which is taken
from *The Chicago Democratic Press:*

"Deacon NORTHAM was one of the few men who
merited, in all respects, the tribute paid by Luke to
Barnabas, 'He was a good man.' Twenty years ago
when a student in Williamstown, Mass., we well remember that he always impressed us with the highest
reverence for his character, as a most worthy represen-
tative of the honest, dignified, noble Puritans. For
many years he had been fully prepared to leave all
things here below, and go to dwell at the right hand
of his Savior.

> " 'His youth was innocent; his riper age
>   Marked with some act of goodness every day;
> And watched by eyes that loved him, calm, and sage
>   Faded his last declining years away;
> Cheerful he gave his being up, and went
>   To share the holy rest, that waits a life well spent.'"

In conclusion we acknowledge our appreciation of
the uniform kindness and assistance which we have
received in gathering the material for this work.

ERRATA.

Page 8, second line from bottom, for "were" read *was*.

Page 10, twelfth and thirteenth lines from top, for "were" read *was*.

Page 18, for "redoutable" read *redoubtable*.

Page 59, in the table, for "Wells and Grant" read *Pierce Downer*.

Page 71, thirteenth line from top, for "are" read *is*.

Other errors of a similar character occur, but as they will not be likely to mislead the reader, it is deemed unnecessary to point them out.

INDEX.

Printed in the United States
122199LV00005B/100/A